Affordable Housing Development

Jaime P. Luque • Nuriddin Ikromov •
William B. Noseworthy

Affordable Housing Development

Financial Feasibility, Tax Increment Financing
and Tax Credits

Jaime P. Luque
ESCP Europe
Madrid, Spain

Nuriddin Ikromov
California State University
Sacramento, CA, USA

William B. Noseworthy
McNeese State University
Lake Charles, LA, USA

ISBN 978-3-030-04063-5   ISBN 978-3-030-04064-2 (eBook)
https://doi.org/10.1007/978-3-030-04064-2

Library of Congress Control Number: 2019933391

© Springer Nature Switzerland AG 2019

This work is subject to copyright. All rights are reserved by the Publisher, whether the whole or part of the material is concerned, specifically the rights of translation, reprinting, reuse of illustrations, recitation, broadcasting, reproduction on microfilms or in any other physical way, and transmission or information storage and retrieval, electronic adaptation, computer software, or by similar or dissimilar methodology now known or hereafter developed.

The use of general descriptive names, registered names, trademarks, service marks, etc. in this publication does not imply, even in the absence of a specific statement, that such names are exempt from the relevant protective laws and regulations and therefore free for general use.

The publisher, the authors and the editors are safe to assume that the advice and information in this book are believed to be true and accurate at the date of publication. Neither the publisher nor the authors or the editors give a warranty, express or implied, with respect to the material contained herein or for any errors or omissions that may have been made. The publisher remains neutral with regard to jurisdictional claims in published maps and institutional affiliations.

This Springer imprint is published by the registered company Springer Nature Switzerland AG
The registered company address is: Gewerbestrasse 11, 6330 Cham, Switzerland

Preface

This book grew out of a major class project that Professor Jaime Luque designed to give students real-world experience in solving problems after the fashion of the teaching style of Professor James A. Graaskamp. Graaskamp, who was a leader, establishing real estate as a field of academic training, consistently emphasized an ethics-based approach to the study, training, teaching, and practice of real estate development. Following upon Graaskamp's inspiration, this course was awarded the prestigious *Ideas Worth Teaching* Award by the Aspen Institute, placing Professor Luque's course among just 20 exceptional peers who led courses in 2018 at top-ranking business programs across Europe, the Middle East, North America, and the Pacific. Most importantly, it was the content of the course, especially that which focused on addressing a local affordable housing crisis, that motivated this award and, indeed, this book. Both students and local community figures from the municipal and county levels saw tremendous benefit from it. As the project grew, and local expert practitioners, as well as an increased number of community members, became involved in the project, we realized there was great value in writing a book specifically about affordable housing development. We hope that the book provides a guide for students, instructors, and practitioners to look at the problem of the lack of affordable housing in mid-sized midwestern cities in the United States through the lens of economists, real estate experts, and potential developers.

Madrid, Spain	Jaime P. Luque
Sacramento, CA	Nuriddin Ikromov
Lake Charles, LA	William B. Noseworthy

Acknowledgements

In this project, we benefited substantially from the intellectual contributions of local policy experts, researchers, and industry experts in urban development. We are particularly grateful for the lectures and interviews that they allowed us to draw upon in the writing of this book. We would especially like to thank Mayor Paul Soglin (City of Madison), Matt Wachter (City of Madison), Karla Thennes (Porchlight), Steve Schooler (Porchlight), David Ginger (WHEDA), Tom Landgraf (Wisconsin School of Business and Dimension Development LLC), Lisa MacKinnon (Dane County), Olivia Parry (Dane County), Todd Violante (Dane County), Rob Dicke (Dane County Housing Authority), Karin Peterson Thurlow (Dane County), Mary Kolar (Dane County), Karyn Knaak (Cinnaire), Chris Jillings (Cinnaire), Katherine Rist (Foley & Lardner LLP), Mike Mooney (MLG Capital), Mike Harrigan (Ehlers), Kristin Rucinski (The Road Home), Ruben Anthony (Urban League), Renee Moe (United Way), Ron Cramer (Wisconsin School of Business), Suzanne Dove (Wisconsin School of Business), Steve Malpezzi (University of Wisconsin-Madison), and Chris Herbert (Joint Center for Housing Studies, Harvard University).

If there are any successes of this project, they lie with the contributions of these individuals. If there are any shortcomings or concerns, the responsibility lies with the authors.

Contents

1	**Housing Affordability Crisis: The United States**	1
	The Case of Madison, Wisconsin	5
	References	11
2	**Homelessness, Housing Public Policy and Urban Planning**	13
	Principles of Need and Creation of Urban Space	13
	Development of Cities	14
	Affordable Housing and Public Policy: Who Pays and Who Benefits? . . .	16
	Where Do We House the Homeless?	18
	The Case of Madison, Wisconsin	21
	The City of Madison's Urban Policy and Development Initiatives	22
	Local Policy At the County Level: Initiatives and Challenges	27
	Conclusion	29
	References	30
3	**The Low-Income Housing Tax Credit (LIHTC) Program**	33
	Introduction to LIHTC	33
	How the LIHTC Program Is Administered at the State Level	37
	WHEDA: How Wisconsin Does LIHTC	39
	WHEDA Scoring and LIHTC Applications	41
	Preparing for the WHEDA Application: Research	42
	How Developers Can Use LIHTC in Practice	42
	Establishing Site Control	44
	Benefits of a Small Firm	46
	Site Control and Zoning: Challenges for the Developer	48
	References	49
4	**The Tax Increment Financing (TIF) Program**	51
	Introduction to TIF	51
	TIF in the United States	52
	Criticisms of the TIF Mechanism	53

	Creation of Tax Increment Districts	55
	The Review Process	58
	TIF from the Developer's Perspective	60
	TIF from the Perspective of Policy Makers	62
	Conclusion	63
	References	64
5	**Housing the Homeless**	65
	Porchlight: An Introduction	65
	Porchlight's Considerations Regarding Housing Location and Size	66
	Porchlight's Considerations Regarding Housing Services	68
	Emergency Shelters	69
	Homeless Veterans	70
	Chronic Homelessness	70
	Breakdown of Homeless Individuals By Household Type in Madison	71
	Free Mobility: Does Madison, WI, Attract Homeless From Other States?	71
	Homeless as a Working Class: Barriers to Access Permanent Housing	73
	Market Rents and Affordable Housing in Madison	74
	The Way to Pay for Services for the Homeless Is to Run Affordable Housing Programs	77
	Homeless Children	78
	Conclusion	79
	Reference	79
6	**Financial Feasibility Analysis: Planning for the Possible**	81
	Graaskamp's Financial Feasibility Model	81
	References	87
7	**Location, Location, Location**	89
	Numerical Example	91
	Development Is Unlikely Without Subsidies	94
	Conclusion	94
	References	97
8	**The Critical Role of TIF, LIHTC, and City Grants**	99
	Financial Feasibility With and Without Subsidies	100
	Tax Increment Financing Usually Does Not Make or Break a Project	101
	Low-Income Housing Tax Credit Can Make a Huge Difference	104
	A Financial Feasibility Model with TIF, LIHTC and City Subsidies	108
	Conclusion	111
	References	112

9	**Affordable Housing Development: Further Considerations for Developers**	113
	Why Non-profit Lenders Are Needed	113
	An Example of a Non-profit Lender	114
	Going Deeper: Cinnaire as an Example of a Lender	116
	Conclusion	120
	References	120
10	**Beyond Financing: The Process of Development**	121
	Developer's Perspective	121
	Madison and Local Need	123
	At the County Level	126
	References	128
References		129

About the Authors

Jaime P. Luque is Associate Professor at ESCP Europe Business School and affiliate of the Center of Financial Security at the University of Wisconsin-Madison. He was previously an Assistant Professor of Real Estate and Urban Economics at the University of Wisconsin-Madison School of Business, where this book was written.

Jaime's current research interests are in affordable housing development, non-prime mortgage lending, and real estate finance and economics in general. His academic research has been published in journals such as the *Journal of Economic Theory*, the *Journal of Public Economics*, the *Journal of Housing Economics*, *Economic Theory*, *Real Estate Economics*, and *Regional Science and Urban Economics*. He has also published three books for business students: *Urban Land Economics* (Springer), *Rays of Research on Real Estate Development* (Business Experts Press), and *The Subprime Crisis: Lessons for Business Students* (World Scientific Publishing).

Jaime's teaching interests include real estate finance, affordable housing, and urban economics. Jaime has teaching experience in both the MBA and BBA programs. Recently, his pedagogical efforts in his urban economics course have focused on the topic of affordable housing development. This module culminated in a "Big Event on Homelessness and Affordable Housing." More than 300 community members, legislators, students, and faculty convened to hear from guest speakers about the state of affordable housing and how the recommendations of the students' projects can make housing more affordable in Madison, Wisconsin.

Jaime has also been deeply involved with the administrative side of the Wisconsin School of Business. He had several positions, including organizing a big conference on the topic of affordable housing and homelessness and promoting a collaboration between the City of Madison and the Wisconsin School of Business on topics such as urban planning and development.

Jaime is the recipient of the 2017 *Ideas Worth Teaching Award* by the Aspen Institute Business and Society Program for his educational innovations to address affordable housing development.

Nuriddin Ikromov is an Associate Professor of Real Estate at the College of Business Administration at California State University, Sacramento. He was a Visiting Professor at Wisconsin School of Business in January 2017—May 2018. His research interests include real estate market efficiency, experimental economics, and housing markets. Nuriddin's papers have been published in the premier academic real estate journals, such as *Real Estate Economics* and *Journal of Real Estate Finance and Economics*. He is a coauthor of the real estate section of the *Sacramento Business Review*, a semiannual publication that provides an economic analysis of the greater Sacramento region.

Nuriddin has taught graduate and undergraduate courses in urban economics, analysis of real estate markets, real estate finance and investments, and real estate fundamentals. He was the winner of the outstanding teaching award at California State University, Sacramento, in 2015. He also served as the faculty director of the Business Honors program at the same school. Nuriddin holds a PhD in real estate finance from the Pennsylvania State University.

William B. Noseworthy is an Assistant Professor in the Department of History at McNeese State University. He was previously a Lecturer at the University of Wisconsin-Madison in the Department of History. He has more than a decade of experience working in both a research and educational capacity with marginalized and low-income populations in Ohio, New York, Wisconsin, Vietnam, Cambodia, and Laos. His research interests include narratives of low-income communities, migrant populations, labor history, land use change, policy, religious minorities, and linguistic minorities. During his dissertation work, he worked with the Cham minority language community in Vietnam and Cambodia, especially with a UNESCO-affiliated research program and the Center for Khmer Studies. He was a founding member of the editorial board of the *Journal of Cham Cultural Studies*, a venue for ground-up research published in Vietnamese. He was coauthor with Sakaya and others on the UNESCO-affiliated Cham language dictionary project which resulted in the first Cham-English-Vietnamese dictionary ever published to use the Cham script. He additionally designed the US Library of Congress standard romanization for Cham script. He has published articles for the *Austrian Journal of Southeast Asian Studies*, the *Journal of Northeast Asian History*, *Asian Highlands Perspectives*, and *Suvannabhumi: Multidisciplinary Journal of Southeast Asian Studies*.

After he returned to the USA, in 2014, he changed his publication style to focus on pedagogical materials. He has since authored many articles and book chapters for ABC-CLIO, ABC-CLIO/Greenwood, and Gale Researcher publications. His teaching has addressed a wide variety of topics, from Asian religions, history of China, history of the Vietnam War, Asian American history, history of the Afro-Atlantic, and history of rap. A substantial portion of the history of rap course included examinations of urban economics in East London, Paris, Rio de Janiero, Havana, Dakar, Tokyo, and Jakarta. He has also been deeply involved in community work in Madison and organized a substantial public symposium on community–police relations in Madison in 2016.

Chapter 1
Housing Affordability Crisis: The United States

Abstract Housing affordability is one of the key parameters that capture the standards of living of the most vulnerable sector of the population in a country. In the United States, access to rental housing has recently been attained one of the lowest levels in the last two decades despite the sustained economic growth of the US economy since 2010. In 2015, almost half of all renters in the United States were cost burdened (i.e., spent at least 30% of their income on housing). The percentage of renters that were severely cost burdened—spent at least half their incomes for housing—was more than a quarter. Figures vary across cities in the United States, with dramatic figures in coastal and non-coastal regions. We review the case of the City of Madison in Wisconsin as an example of a mid-west city with serious housing affordability problems but strong economic fundamentals.

Housing affordability is arguably the most critical housing issue in the United States today. Compared to other housing problems, such as physically inadequate housing, homelessness, racial segregation and discrimination, affordability adversely affects the welfare of a much more significant number of households. These problems are not distinct. They are interrelated with issues of housing affordability. As Quigley and Raphael (2004) point out, housing is the single largest budget item for most households. Furthermore, while households spend about a quarter of their incomes on housing on average, poor households often spend more than half their incomes. Therefore, relatively small percentage changes in rents can have an outsized effect on low-income families' welfare.

Housing is considered unaffordable if the household must spend "too much" on housing. In the United States, the most commonly used threshold is 30% of income, in part due to its use by the Department of Housing and Urban Development. As Green and Malpezzi (2003) point out, this rule is not strictly economic—if a household is currently spending 40% of its income on housing, then by definition it can afford it. However, it is sensible to argue that affordability is related to the share of household income spent on housing and that the higher is this share, the less resources the household has for other necessary expenditures (e.g., food, transportation, schooling, medications, and other basic needs). While the 30% rule is arbitrary, it is not unreasonable. In some cases, researchers also use a 50% cutoff.

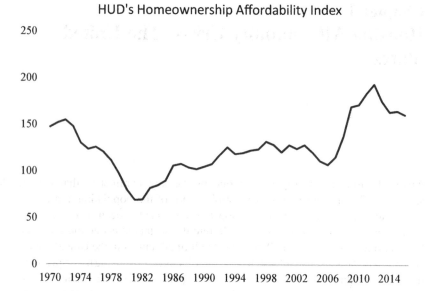

Fig. 1.1 The annual homeownership affordability index produced by the Department of Housing and Urban Development. Higher index values indicate that homeownership is more affordable

We start by documenting the decline in housing affordability, particularly for renters, which is our focus of this book. Some organizations and agencies produce measures of affordability of owner-occupied housing. Two well-known are the National Association of Realtors (NAR) "Housing affordability index" and the U.S. Department of Housing and Urban Development's (HUD) "Homeownership affordability index".[1] The latter, presented in Fig. 1.1, is the ratio of median family income to the income required to qualify for a conventional mortgage to buy the median-valued house. The index is equal to 100 if the median family earns just enough income to buy a median-priced home. Higher (lower) index levels indicate that housing is more (less) affordable.

Quigley and Raphael (2004) point out that homeownership was as affordable in 2000 as it was in 1970. Indeed, the chart shows that owning a home in the United States was slightly more affordable in 2016 than in 1970, short-to-medium fluctuations notwithstanding. The median family earned about 60% more income than was required to purchase a median-priced home in 2016, a little higher than the 50% difference in 1970. Affordability peaked in 2012 (index value was 193), as housing markets reached their post-bubble troughs, and mortgage rates remained historically

---

[1] There is a debate on what is the best housing affordability index. See for example Glaeser and Gyourko (2003), who propose the alternative affordability index of the ratio between house prices and housing construction costs. They argue that "a housing affordability crisis means that housing is expensive relative to its fundamental costs of production—not that people are poor" (Glaeser and Gyourko 2003, p. 21).

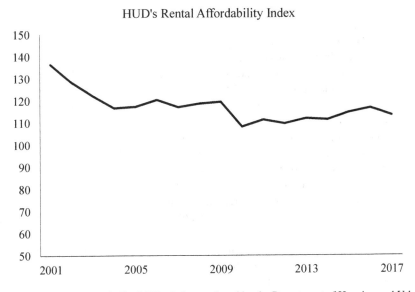

Fig. 1.2 The annual rental affordability index produced by the Department of Housing and Urban Development. Higher index values indicate that renting is more affordable

low. Prices have since significantly appreciated in most markets, reducing affordability in the last 4 years. Although homeownership seems relatively affordable on this basis, it is important to note that the index calculated based upon a national average. Homeownership is much more difficult to achieve in many relatively expensive metropolitan areas.

While it is informative to review the historical affordability of homeownership, our focus here is rental housing. HUD has more recently created index tracks rental affordability. It is calculated based upon the ratio of 30% of median renter household income to the median rent. The 30% threshold is used for many government assistance programs, as well as by most landlords. The rental affordability index equals 100 if the median renter household earns just enough income to be able to afford the median-rent unit. Figure 1.2 shows HUD's annual rental affordability index, which only goes back to 2001.

The chart shows the evident decline in rental affordability over the last 16 years. In 2001, the median renter household in the United States earned 40% more income than was enough to rent the median rental unit. In the third quarter of 2017, this number had fallen to 112—a 20% decline in affordability. Again, note that the index is calculated for the entire country. In many large cities, more than half of renter households are rent-burdened, meaning they spend more than 30% of their incomes on rent. Even so, the index likely overstates rental affordability. As the homeownership fell from a high of 69% in 2004 to 64% in 2017, many households who were previous owners have become renters, boosting the median income of renter households. The fact that the index is calculated for the entire country masks the rent burden in relative expensive housing markets. In many large cities, more than half of renter households are rent-burdened, meaning they spend more than 30% of their incomes on rent.

While HUD's rental affordability index goes back to only 2001, low-income households rent burden has been rising for decades. While HUD's rental affordability index goes back to only 2000, low-income households rent burden has been growing for decades. For example, Malpezzi and Green (1996) cite evidence that the number of very-low-income households who paid more than half of their income on rent increased from 24% in 1974 to more than 40% two decades later.

As one would expect, the affordable housing problem is primarily one of rent burden.[2] According to the most recent housing report by Harvard's Joint Center for Housing Studies, almost half of all renters were cost burdened (i.e., spent at least 30% of their income on housing) in 2015. The problem was even more acute for lower-income households: 83% of renters with incomes under $15,000, and 77% of renters with incomes between $15,000 and $29,999 were cost burdened. More than a quarter of renters spent at least half their incomes for housing (Joint Center 2017).

The evidence from the Joint Center for Housing Studies is consistent with the evidence in the study by Gyourko et al. (2013) on superstar cities. The authors show that some so-called "superstar" cities experienced persistent high price appreciation between 1950 and 2000, due to those cities' inelastic supply of land and the increase in the number of high-income households nationwide. High house prices in the superstar cities inevitably crowded out lower income households. Therefore, the housing affordability problem is particularly severe in superstar cities.

Currently, affordability is a particularly acute problem in the large cities on the East and West coasts of the United States, in places like New York City, Boston, Los Angeles, San Francisco, and Seattle. Particularly in California, the rising cost of housing has been forcing tens of thousands of residents to move to other states where housing is less expensive. According to an analysis by Legislative Analyst's Office (California legislature's nonpartisan fiscal and policy advisor), between 2007 and 2016 the net migration into the state was negative 1 million. Five million people moved into California from other states, while 6 million Californians left for other states (Uhler and Garosi 2018). Not surprisingly, people who leave the state tend to have lower incomes, while people who move in earn much higher wages. Between 2005 and 2015, net migration into California was negative 800,000 for people close to the official poverty line, while the state gained 20,000 earning at least five times the poverty rate.[3] The top three destinations for people leaving California were Texas, Arizona, and Nevada, all states with relatively low house prices. In contrast, people who moved to California tend to come from states where housing is relatively expensive, such as New York, Illinois, and New Jersey.

---

[2]Quigley and Raphael (2004) point out that improvements in the quality of rental units due to changes in income, tastes and government regulations that mandate minimum quality housing standards also help explain the increasing rent burden. However, decreases in the median income of renter households have been responsible for the majority of the increase in rent burden.

[3]See Reese, Philip 3/5/2017. California exports its poor to Texas, other states, while wealthier people move in. *Sacramento Bee*.

High and rising house prices not only affect the economies of the economies of individual regions but can have a ripple effect on the country as a whole. The most apparent result for the affected area is that large numbers of families are uprooted, disrupting social connections and children's education [see *Evicted: Poverty and Profit in the American City* (2016) by Matthew Desmond and *Hillbilly Elegy* (2016) by J. D. Vance]. Also, high house prices mean that employers higher wages to their workers. Since labor costs are a significant part of the overall cost of production, higher wages raise the prices of locally produced goods and services. Higher costs make the region's economy less competitive and ultimately hurts its potential to grow. Furthermore, if house prices in an area become high enough, the resulting exodus can increase housing demand in neighboring cities, thereby putting upward pressure on house prices in those regions as well. In fact, increased demand from people leaving California's booming housing market is already pushing prices up, causing traffic congestion, and raising tensions in communities in nearby Nevada, Arizona, and Utah.[4]

High house prices also have implications for income inequality in the United States. Recent research by Raj Chetty and his co-authors explores how the upward mobility of children from low-income families is correlated with where they grow up (Chetty et al. 2014). They find that upward mobility varies widely by the city and neighborhood. Most relevant for our purposes, the top eight cities where children from low-income families are more likely to move up in the income distribution are: San Jose, San Francisco, Washington DC, Seattle, Salt Lake City, New York, Boston, and San Diego. With the possible exception of Salt Lake City, these are all markets with extremely high median house prices. In other words, the cities where a poor child has the best chance to move up the income ladder are also the cities with the highest house prices. Therefore, the astronomically high house prices in places like Northern California, New York, Boston and Washington DC are in a way perpetuating income inequality in our society.

The Case of Madison, Wisconsin

While it is most visible in the large coastal cities, housing affordability is a growing problem in many parts of the country, particularly in cities with robust economies. The City of Madison in Wisconsin is a good example. Madison is the capital of Wisconsin and is located in Dane County, in South Central part of the state. The City of Madison is home to over 250,000 people, while the larger Madison metropolitan area has a population of about 600,000. The city is home to the flagship campus of the University of Wisconsin system. According to the Affordable Housing Market Report, in the City of Madison 50% of renters pay more than 30% of their income in rent (housing cost burdened). The percentage of severely housing cost burdened (pay more than 50% of their income in rent) is an alarming 30%. Homelessness is also

---

[4]See Dougherty (2018) and Mathews (2017).

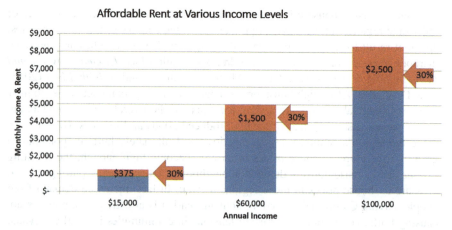

Fig. 1.3 Maximum affordable rents at various income levels, using the 30% affordability criterion. Source: City of Madison Biennial Housing Report, HUD

present in Madison, with 3000–4000 people being served annually by the shelter system 1 in 3 are children. These harsh realities contrast with its solid economic growth in the last years and a striking transformation from a government-based economy to a more diversified system with consumer services and a growing high-tech industry. Throughout the rest of the chapter, we document the extent of the affordability challenges in the City of Madison, Wisconsin.

The following discussion elaborates on the Madison's housing affordability figures and problems. Most insights were obtained from the Biennial Housing Report, written by the city's housing initiatives specialist. Using the 30% of income rate as the threshold, Fig. 1.3 shows the maximum monthly rent a household can afford at various income levels. At the 30% rate, affordable housing for a single person working a full-time position at minimum wage, earning an income of $15,000/year, would be a rent of $375/month. For middle income, someone earning $60,000/year, they could afford $1500/month in housing costs. For someone making $100,000/year, they would be comfortable with $2500/month in housing costs.

The figure shows that for households earning $60,000 or more, affordability is not a major problem, because the average market rent for a 2-bedroom apartment is below $1500 in Madison. On the other hand, households with annual incomes of less than $50,000 could spend much of their incomes on housing.

Some of the most common occupations in Madison are: customer service representative (annual wages: $33,940), cashier ($19,830), janitor ($25,800), laborer ($26,730), waiter/waitress ($20,600), and administrative assistant ($35,340). So a large share of the labor force is earning $35,000 or less working full time. The simple fact is that housing places a very high-cost burden on many workers in the city.

Figure 1.4 shows numbers of households by income range in Madison in 2010. The figure shows that about 46% of all households faced possible affordability issues. This share is over 60% when we consider only renter households. One caveat

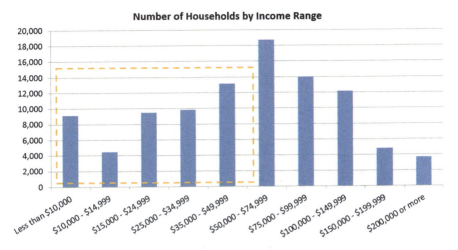

Fig. 1.4 Number of households by income in Madison. Source: City of Madison Biennial Housing Report, 2010 Decennial Census

	2000 Census to 2007 ACS		2007 ACS to 2015 ACS	
	Annual Growth Rate	Total Growth	Annual Growth Rate	Total Growth
Population	1%	7%	1.5%	12%
Households	0.0%	0%	2%	20%
Renter Households	-2%	-14%	4.5%	43%
Owner Households	2%	15%	0%	0%

Fig. 1.5 Growth rates for population, total, renter, and owner household in Madison, WI from 2000 to 2015. Source: American Community Housing Survey, City of Madison

is that many University of Wisconsin students do not work, and will show up as having zero income in the data, even if they come from affluent families and have no affordability issues. However, even if we exclude the lowest income group (income less than $10,000, which is 9% of all households), over 50% of renter households are potentially rent-burdened.

The population growth in the City of Madison has been steady for decades, at an incremental increase of just 1% per year, even during the Great Recession of 2007–2009. However, this does not mean that the recession had no impact on the housing market. From 1950 until the Great Recession, virtually all growth had been in homeowners. However, since 2007, the number of homeowners has not changed, and all of the household growth has been from renters. As Fig. 1.5 shows, from 2007 to 2015 the number of renter households in Madison grew by 17,000, or 43%.

The common perception is that much of this growth has been from millennials moving to the city to work in large firms and corporations, such as Epic, tech firms, and biotech research firms. This impression is generally accurate. However, after the recession, growth has also all been in either the low and high-income households,

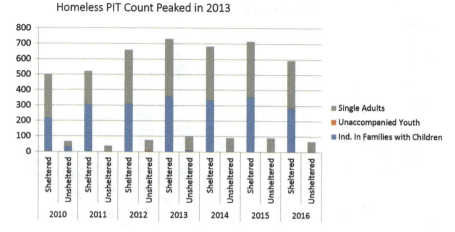

Fig. 1.6 Homeless population statistics for Madison, WI, 2010—2016. Source: Point in Time Count

with no increase in between. Furthermore, there has been a tremendous jump in need of rental units, 5000 since 2007. The city has just not been able to keep up with this dramatic increase in demand. About half of the renters are spending a reliable 30% of their income on rent now. However, there are currently 7000–8000 non-students who are spending half of their monthly income or more on rent each month, and this incremental increase in the housing vulnerable population is not related to the recession, it seems, but long-term deeper structural trends. All of this highlights the critical need for additional housing, particularly affordable housing. Solutions and strategies for the City of Madison model align city, state and federal initiatives. The city pursues the strategy of proactively seeking partnerships with private developers.

As far as the City of Madison has been concerned, the number one housing problem in the city has been a problem of homelessness, which peaked in 2013, but seems to have receded, in part thanks to local initiatives (Soglin et al. 2013). Figure 1.6 shows the numbers of homeless adults, unaccompanied youths, and individuals in families with children in Madison in the years 2010–2016.

The city has targeted hardest to serve populations, build housing just for that group of people. Housing for people to get them out of housing and then into an apartment. Currently homeless shelters are in old school gymnasiums and church basements. But now, the city focuses on permanent supportive housing.

The most prominent example of this focus is Rethke Terrace, a project with 60 studio apartments, partly funded with $1.45 million in City Affordable Housing Funds. The building is one of the most sustainable multi-family buildings in the Midwest, being LEED Platinum and PassiveHouse certified. The project targets the most vulnerable and chronically homeless families, offering them 24/7 staffing, onsite social services staff. It was built as a collaborative project between a non-profit real estate developer and a non-profit healthcare provider.

The process of the construction plan was lengthy but short by urban planning standards. First, the City of Madison optioned a site three blocks from a free clinic and a robust bus line. Next, they recruited developers from across the mid-west and selected a team from Chicago to work on the project. They operated on the model that: *Any dollar going to pay for the debt is a dollar less for social services.* The total development cost was $8.9 million, or $149,000 per unit. Since the residents will require extensive services throughout their lives, it is important that such a project has as little debt service as possible. With that in mind, the capital stack for Rethke Terrace's development budget included: $5.6 million in Low Income Housing Tax Credits, $1.45 million in City Affordable Housing Funds, $900,000 in County Funds, $850,000 in Affordable Housing Program grants from the Federal Home Loan Bank of Chicago, as well as money raised through a private fundraising campaign. This shows how difficult it can be to fund housing for the homeless that also offers necessary services.

Although the building has no debt service, it still requires about $500,000 in cash flow to pay for staffing and social services. Since the residents do not have any income, they are unable to pay any rent. The city solved this problem by using Section 8 vouchers. Another gap filler was Medicaid reimbursement for the state. The unit has been incredibly successful by city standards, and 57/60 individuals remained after 1 year: one has passed away, and another two moved on to some other form of housing. Because this model was so successful, the city now has another unit under construction on the West Side under a partnership with the YWCA. There is a contemporary question of how potential federal changes to services funding could impact the services partnered model at the state and municipal levels. In the case we consider, the model applies for the relatively stable pre-funding through Medicaid HMO program, as opposed to the more threatened CCS program, and there is optimism that this will keep the services insulated from any federal shifts to service funding.

After the homeless, the next most vulnerable population in the City of Madison is the low-income renters. Our research suggests the projected city level need is 1500–2000 new apartments needed per year, with at least half of these units being affordable housing. Since the recession hit, 100–200 units have been added per year at most.

The vacancy rate in the Madison housing market has been much lower than the benchmark 5% equilibrium level for the vacancy rate in the United States for at least a decade. As Fig. 1.7 shows, vacancy dropped from 6% in 2005 to 1.9% in 2013. As of the first quarter of 2017, the vacancy rate in Madison was around 3%, which is still much lower than the 5% equilibrium level. A 3% vacancy is not suitable for renters, especially those in the low-income category.[5]

---

[5]This 3% vacancy may be understated, since vacancy is measured by the local electric utility's meters. In a building with multiple units but with a common meter, the entire structure is counted as fully occupied as long as the meter is running.

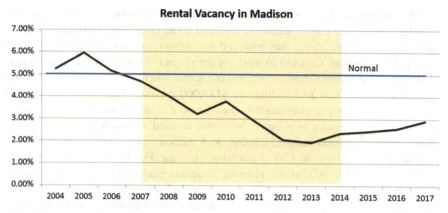

Fig. 1.7 Rental vacancy in Madison, WI, the first quarter of 2004—first quarter of 2017. Source: City of Madison Biennial Housing Report, Madison Gas, and Electric

Fig. 1.8 The average listed rents for 1 bedroom and 2 bedroom units in Madison. Source: rentjungle.com

The low vacancy rate puts landlords in a strong bargaining position. As a result, tenants may have a harder time finding and securing an apartment. This is especially true for low-income households, who are more likely to have poor credit histories or have an eviction on their record. Also, low vacancy rates typically lead to higher rents. Not surprisingly, just after the recession, as a direct result of the low vacancy rate, monthly rent for a two-bedroom apartment also increased dramatically, from around $900 in 2012 to almost $1500 by the end of 2016. This trend is evident in Fig. 1.8, which shows average listed rents for one bedroom and two bedroom apartments in Madison from 2009 to 2016.

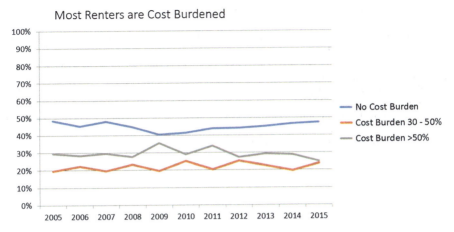

Fig. 1.9 The shares of renters with different rent-to-income ratios in Madison, WI. Source: 1-Year American Community Survey

The combination of a considerable number of workers who do not earn high wages but pay high (and rising) rents means that a significant portion of renters are cost-burdened. We conclude this chapter by showing, in Fig. 1.9, that more than half of all renters in Madison spend at least 30% of their income on rent, and that about a quarter of renters spend at least half their income on rent.

The recent serious strains in the US housing market at both the national and regional levels are moving the debate towards finding public policies that can effectively make housing more affordable for the most vulnerable populations. In the following chapters, we review the most important public policies and provide an analytical economic framework to assess their effectiveness.

References

Chetty R, Hendren N, Kline P, Saez E (2014) Where is the land of opportunity? The geography of intergenerational mobility in the United States. Q J Econ 129(4):1553–1623

Desmond M (2016) Evicted: poverty and profit in the American City. Crown, New York

Dougherty C (2018, March 20) California housing problems are spilling across its borders. New York Times

Glaeser EL, Gyourko JE (2003) The impact of building restrictions on housing affordability. Econ Policy Rev 9(2):21–39

Green RK, Malpezzi S (2003) A primer on us housing markets and housing policy. AREUEA monograph series. Urban Institute Press, Washington, DC

Gyourko J, Mayer C, Sinai T (2013) Superstar cities. Am Econ J Econ Policy 5(4):167–199

Joint Center for Housing Studies of Harvard University (2017) The state of the Nation's housing. Harvard University, Cambridge, MA

Malpezzi S, Green RK (1996) What has happened to the bottom of the US housing market? Urban Stud 33(10):1807–1820

Mathews J (2017, July 3) California's housing crisis is spreading to other states. San Francisco Chronicle

Quigley JA, Raphael S (2004) Is housing unaffordable? Why isn't it more affordable? J Econ Perspect 18(1):191–214

Reese P (2017, March 5) California exports its poor to Texas, other states, while wealthier people move in. Sacramento Bee

Soglin P, O'Keefe J, Wallinger S, Rhodes L (2013) Annual report on homeless persons served in Dane County. City of Madison

Uhler B, Garosi J (2018) California losing residents via domestic migration. California legislative analyst's office report

Vance JD (2016) Hillbilly Elegy. Harper Press, New York

Chapter 2
Homelessness, Housing Public Policy and Urban Planning

Abstract This chapter focuses on the nature of urban spaces in the field of policy. We begin with the basic principles of need created through urban areas and examining how urban spaces are created, before turning to the question of how cities develop. We consider the question of who pays and who benefits in the case of affordable housing policy from a theoretical and practical perspective. We additionally discuss the question of where to house inevitable homeless population found in any large urban space and give space to assess the broader need for affordable housing extending well beyond the homeless population of a given metropolitan area. In this examination, we focus on Madison, Wisconsin, and the local need in the case of the demand for affordable housing in Midwestern cities. We then turn to the practical solutions that policymakers pursue at the municipal and county levels. Given that these perspectives are often entirely different, but developers across the country will face similar situations of working with both municipal and county level governance, we consider both aspects carefully. We explore the perspectives of both urban and suburban management into conversation with each other, to provide developers, industry experts, academics, and public officials a means to continue the discussion. Our approach in this chapter is straightforward, but carefully considers the difficulties that mainly municipal and local policymakers face, along with pointing towards ways that developers could begin to unveil creative solutions to address the needs of the affordable housing market.

Principles of Need and Creation of Urban Space

Most people understand that there is a principle of the hierarchy of needs. To have a car move you need to put gas in the car. To have a laborer work, that laborer must be housed and fed. In his 1943 paper "A Theory of Human Motivation," Abraham Maslow argued that there was a hierarchy of needs for each human. Self-actualization, such as thinking, learning, and fulfillment was at the top of his hierarchy, while physical and environmental requirements, such as community, housing, food, and healthcare were at the bottom. If these most basic needs are not satisfied, it is difficult or impossible to pursue higher needs (Maslow 1943). Like

Maslow's concept of the hierarchy of needs, we can think of five critical elements to the survival of an urban community. They are housing, transportation, childcare, education/skills and training, and healthcare. Healthcare includes the sub-categories of nutrition, mental health care, and substance abuse, which are elements of the urban community that are often ignored. The question facing urban developers is: *What good does it do for an individual to have one, or even four, of these elements if they do not have access to just one?* Removing access to only one of the five elements can remove the individual from the labor force.

Take one of the elements: transportation. As a thought experiment, we might ask: *why emphasize transportation? What is so important about it?* Well, we could think of any prosperous city that is a desirable location. Consider some of the great cities of the world, such as Barcelona, Paris, Boston, Chicago, Sydney, London, Miami, Budapest, or Dublin. What do they all have in common? The foundation of the city is the market. It is commerce. These are all gateway cities. They are harbors, or entry points to intersections at water-cross roads, as well as in the foothills. Still, what they have in common is commerce. Each of these examples was historically critical for the transportation of goods or ideas. Each one of them was a city that was teeming with companies trading products, pirates pillaging, and poets professing their latest fancies. They were built at the crossroads of the marketplace.

Development of Cities

The most basic needs of an urban environment are transportation and shelter. Adequate housing and transportation are always top priorities for urban planning in the realm of policy. Moreover, part of the problem with downtown environs, from the perspective of policymakers, is that there will always be a class of poor people in the city. Although it is undoubtedly the case that theorists have imagined ways to attempt to create spaces where wealth is shared, the eradication of poverty has not been possible in any historical example of an urban environment. But where does poverty originate? Where do the more impoverished populations of urban areas come from? The prominent urban economist Edward Glaeser argues that *"Cities aren't full of poor people because cities make people poor, but because cities attract poor people with the prospect of improving their lot in life."*[1] Cities have historically attracted people because of the potential for a safer environment or job prospects, or other services, such as education and healthcare. In the case of many large cities in the developing world, such as Lagos and Rio de Janeiro, people are attracted to cities with high crime rates and poverty because conditions in rural areas are often even worse.

In the United States, the dynamics of job opportunities, crime, healthcare, and other services are somewhat different. Particularly in the Midwest, significant

---

[1] Glaeser (2011).

motivation for low-income families moving to mid-sized cities in this region would be a combination of safety (in the case of families moving from parts of large Midwestern cities with comparatively high violent crime rates, such as Chicago, Indianapolis, Detroit or Milwaukee), and job prospects (in the case of virtually all individuals).

As the population of a city grows, public policymakers worry about absorbing the newcomers into the city's economy and housing markets, as well as to make sure that the city's transportation system can accommodate the larger population. The migrant population will always need a place to live, and, very often, that place will need to be close to public transportation. The priority is to make housing available and affordable. If not, cities will be unable to absorb the growing population, restricting the labor force, increasing wages and production costs, and ultimately choking off economic activity.

A commonly used rule of thumb suggests that 30% of income should go to housing. If that number increases significantly, the increased financial stress on the individual or family will be dramatic. So, how do we make up the difference? Should the federal government subsidize the cost? Should the state? Should the city? With the consideration of each possible scenario, it is critical to ask: *who makes up the difference in cost?* Also: *who benefits from the potential development model?*

Before moving on to housing in more detail, it would make sense to consider the simpler model of public transportation. Let us consider again the City of Madison in Wisconsin, as an example. The City invests tens of millions of dollars for road improvements and bike paths, over multiple year cycles, even for small projects, such as a nearly $20 million improvement of the Johnson Street corridor. The costs of bike paths, roads, buses, bus stations and more are enormous. This should not be surprising. One should not expect that there is a single public transportation system in the United States that pays for itself.[2]

In the city of Madison, suppose the per-use cost of a trip is four dollars. The individual, however, only pays two dollars per ride for the bus, meaning the city's bus transit system (Metro) runs a deficit. Who subsidizes the difference? *Who pays?* Indeed, some of the funds come from the University of Wisconsin-Madison's segregated fees structures. But, much more significantly, most of the resources are derived from the tax base of the city.

Who benefits? The people who benefit are the riders naturally. Although most analyses of public transportation stop the benefit at the passengers, we know they are not the only beneficiaries. The employees of the transit system also benefit. Other employees in the city benefit from a decrease in traffic congestion. There is less pollution, which is vital for the public, but also for the public employees whose task it is to clean the city. Another major group of beneficiaries is the employers. When

---

[2]It is well known that most public transportation systems in the United States are not profitable. In many cases, debt becomes unsustainable and the public transportation system requires government support. This is the case of the Metropolitan Transportation Authority's (MTA) in the city of New York, whose debt as of 2016 was above $25 billion (more than the debt of many small nations).

public transit system is convenient and reliable, employers do not need to spend as much money on maintaining parking, building expensive parking ramps, maintaining lots, and spending money on personnel to staff the lots. Furthermore, employers within the city benefit from having a more mobile labor force.

There are many cost-benefit analyses out there that look at transportation for the public as a loser. But these analyses are done inside the silo of public transit. Instead, we should assess the broader benefits for the economy. If we evaluate the more comprehensive benefits of the system, maintaining a healthy public transportation system, well-kept roads, and encouraging the use of alternative transportation through the construction and maintenance of an excellent network of bike paths is ultimately the mark of successful urban planning. For housing, also, it is important not to think inside the silo, but to consider the broader benefits of the system.

Affordable Housing and Public Policy: Who Pays and Who Benefits?

In the case of housing, who pays and who benefits when new houses are built? The answer seems obvious—it is the developer, who buys the land and funds the construction (and expects to earn a profit). However, affordable housing is usually subsidized, through the use of federal tax credits and city subsidies. Who benefits in this scenario? Well, it is possible to suggest that in most analyses the renters are viewed as a group that benefits, although, to be more nuanced, they are not the group that stands to benefit the most from the exchange. Most often the landlord and the developer stand to benefit the most. However, thinking outside the silo, if a housing development is successful, the consideration of the benefits should extend to the broader community. The city itself benefits from housing if the housing is affordable because affordable housing reduces the homeless population. If the housing has the potential to have services attached to the development, such as a community center, the broader community benefits. If the housing development has a daycare, or another form of childcare, such as after-school programming, attached to the location, the more comprehensive community benefits substantially. Housing youth during Out of School Time (OST), while their parents are simultaneously working second or third shift positions comes at a substantial potential cost. But a development that provides proper conditions for low-cost OST to be covered within the development structure is a considerable benefit to the entire neighborhood, and indeed, the whole city.

Without a doubt, one of the biggest problems urban policymakers face is homelessness. What is the problem with large numbers of people living on the street? First and foremost, there is the moral issue of a wealthy society having to provide basic shelter to its most vulnerable members. Beyond that, on a practical level, the homeless are more vulnerable to health conditions. They require care, increasing the cost of public services. Some analysts have suggested that homeless populations are more likely to have criminal convictions (with numbers up to 33%). However, it is also important to keep in mind that homeless people are often policed more strictly than housed populations. Only 13% of surveyed single men (usually a group stereotyped as being the most likely to have a criminal history) self-reported their criminal history as the primary cause of their homelessness in Madison in 2013. 11% reported having stayed the previous night in jail or prison.[3] Still, the potential for petty and more substantial crime among homeless population is not negligible. Homeless populations are also much more vulnerable targets for petty crimes, abuse, and violent crimes. Substance abuse and mental health problems are staggering among the homeless populations that even mid-sized Midwestern cities are working with. Furthermore, the environment can make homeless populations particularly vulnerable. In warmer climates, natural disasters such as hurricanes make homeless populations more exposed. In places such as Arizona, heat waves always hit homeless populations hard. In the case of Midwestern cities, it is the winter. Wind chill coupled with far below freezing temperatures for months out of the year cripple the homeless population of the Midwest. The cost of public services is substantial. There has been a decades-long perspective on municipal policy that holds: if it is possible to house the homeless population, the costs of services will proportionally decline. This is the principle behind the approach to reduce homelessness known as *Housing First*.

Of the many problems of homelessness, stereotyping the homeless population hampers their access to resources. But it also has very real impacts on property values. Large visible homeless populations tend to lower property values since the value of a property is ultimately a factor of perception weighted against reality. Hence, the *Housing First* initiative has attempted, for decades, to treat the problems associated with homeless populations by getting them off the street and into adequate housing. *Housing First* decreases the risk that they will be the targets of crime, that homeless people will become victims of weather, that they will require costly emergency medical care, and create a pathway toward a more stable, higher quality, life. In traditional models of housing the homeless population, the method has made public housing conditional upon a clean record and moving past substance abuse problems. Instead, the *Housing First* method holds that defeating substance abuse and maintaining a cleaner record will be possible if the individual has housing. Furthermore, we know that there is a high correlation for children between the frequency of moving and academic performance. In other words, a child that is homeless is much more likely to remain homeless for an extended period. Hence, *Housing First* is particularly crucial for families who are currently or in danger of becoming homeless.

---

[3]Soglin et al. (2013).

Where Do We House the Homeless?

Having established the need for *Housing First*, the next step in the development process is deciding which population is going to be housed, how to target them, and where they will be housed. Policy makers recognize that we are a highly mobile society and that in most communities, particularly large cities, the homeless population frequently are individuals who were from other areas. They are impacted most significantly, then, by the two principal variables of weather and the quality of public services for those most in need. Many policymakers take the position that if you have a great variety of public services, the weather will become less of a variable. Hypothetically, we could imagine a scenario where one state, for example, South Dakota, does not have excellent services for their homeless population. If so, the homeless of South Dakota would be inclined to migrate. We could hypothesize that some of them would be motivated to move to warmer climes, say California, but others might be driven to move to a city with better amenities than their current location, to follow great services. In this scenario, a segment of the population would be moving across state lines. In fact, we know that homeless populations have often moved across state lines historically. That would make homelessness a federal issue because when commerce (in this case a potential labor force) crosses state lines, it becomes a national responsibility. However, this is not the case currently with housing. Instead, it is primarily the responsibility of individual municipalities, and, occasionally state governments.

Historically, there was federal recognition of a housing crisis linked to the Great Depression, leading to the establishment of national agencies to provide and regulate housing. By the 1950s the balance of responsibility shifted to urban areas and municipal governments. Jane Jacobs held that the metropolitan planning policy was inadequately prepared for this shift and that the lack of appropriate urban planning policy led to the decline of many city neighborhoods in the United States.[4] However, Jacobs was not the only vital author to critique the policies of urban planning. In his book *City: Rediscovering the Center* (1988), which was republished in 2012, the sociologist William H. Whyte included some fundamental analyses of the usage of urban space that are unforgettable. Whyte wrote about the attraction to water, essential for the case of Madison, as the downtown area is situated between a cluster of lakes. But, water was not the only element of the urban environment to which Whyte paid substantial attention. He drew readers' attention to spaces large and small, such as the importance of bench space in creating a friendly urban environment. In a famous experiment, he stuck two individuals on a corner in New York City and had them "accidentally" bump into people and block them from their walking paths as commuters. He found in the experiment that most of the walkers apologized for having someone else bump into them. The experiment was an indicator that when individuals are on the street in a city, they often presume that even minor misfortunes are their fault, as opposed to structural problems. In another

---

[4]Jacobs (1961).

example, he observed space on the window-sills of a bank. The windows faced the sun at noon, so space made excellent impromptu benches for people on their lunch breaks from work. The bank was upset about this, so they put spikes on the window-sills to prevent the space from being used. Just a short time later, Whyte found that artists had come to space and hung their work up for sale, using the spikes that the bank had provided for them as impromptu hooks. Whyte's lesson was: if you have a great space, it will be used no matter what. Whyte's thinking is the type of reasoning that informs the "Global Placemaking Movement," which aims to refine cityscapes into areas of better public interaction for the sake of producing healthier urban communities.

Contemporary theories of urban development sharply contrast with the traditional methods of federally funded housing projects. The traditional approaches suggested that public housing did not need to be of the highest quality. In fact, most public housing projects were deliberately built to be uncomfortable and in inferior locations, so that people would have an incentive to move in when only when they were in a desperate situation, and a strong incentive to move out as soon as possible. The climate of the 1980s, which Whyte was writing in, was a climate of reform, however. Over time, federal housing policy shifted from supply-side policies (primarily construction of public housing) to also include demand-side policies. Chief among these is the Section 8 housing voucher program. The vouchers could be taken to a landlord and exchanged for rent. However, because of the nature of Section 8, the housing was not much better than the federal housing projects. Section 8 housing was often located in areas close to the federal projects, which lacked services. The lack of a tax base meant that the neighborhoods had no access to public schools that were well funded. There was little access to shopping or services that provided primary health care needs.

Next, there was further reform of this concept through the creation of a tax credit-based program using federal funds that are administered by the states. In this program, developers would find a site, create a proposal and receive approval for that plan. But there is also an alternative model to the tax credit-based federal system that focuses on approval of developed plans. This alternative *identifies the sites first*. The municipality ranks the sites in this alternative model, based on the access to public transportation, shopping in the neighborhood, walkability to schools and parks, relative closeness to employment opportunities. After the sites are identified by the city, then the call for projects and proposals is sent out to developers. There has been a complaint statewide that certain cities receive disproportionate credits from the state under this model. In response to this criticism, some people argue that this is the model that has proven superior, and so those that are criticizing the system should perhaps follow this model. The challenge then becomes one of placemaking and providing a high level of services to the areas of new developments.

If the developer succeeds in creating excellent urban space, the people will use it. If you build it, they will come. And vacancies will be low. The secondary challenge, then, becomes the challenge of how to provide a high level of services. For example, if there is a shelter that addresses the needs of individuals who have been on the streets for 25 plus years, that shelter will have to think about what types of services are provided and what the needs of the population they serve are. Substance abuse, chronic unemployment, and primary healthcare, including mental healthcare services, are all, statistically, circumstances that the development will face. Let's say we take an individual who has been on the streets for his entire life. *Do we provide housing? What else do we do?* We make sure that the individual is signed up for every single state and federal subsidy program available because most cities do not have sufficient resources. For example, we provide all types of Medicaid, to bring on a therapist or other individual who can oversee case management. *How do issues become more involved with a family of five?* Childcare and Out of School Time (OST) become needs, especially if there is a transition to employment for the primary caretakers in the family, and even more so if that work is in second and third shift positions.

There is no doubt that the affordable housing crisis is a problem that crosses state lines. It needs federal, state, and municipal policies and resources to be solved, and we need to exploit all the available services. As a thought experiment, let's return to the thought about some of the most significant cities in the world. Consider Barcelona. Consider Paris. *Where do people want to be in the city?* In Paris, inevitably, it is the left bank. It is the marketplace, the most pleasant and bustling part of the city, which for hundreds of years has been more than just a place to pick up your fruits and vegetables. It is a space of public interaction. In cities, the importance of the area is a place of communication. One of the services that are provided is from open space. Because of municipal policy, many cities in the Midwest do not have row houses. However, in many older cities in America, such as Boston, Brooklyn, and Baltimore, there are row houses that provide excellent public space: the front stoops. The open space is essential because of the way that the area acts. In Chicago, this concept is important as well. For example, the row houses provide a means to watch over youth. As one caretaker from Chicago recently said in 2017, "*What we do is simple. We sit on the corners and watch over the children in the neighborhood.*"[5] What happens, though, if you remove that space for such social interaction to take place? We must think about the nature of the social interaction. In the case of Chicago, new modern tenements were built, some 20 stories high, set in an open place. They replaced series of buildings with steps and porches, where was public life. In the tenements, people went into their cubicles.

Placemaking is not limited to housing. Quality of life in cities also depends on clean air and water, as well as things like traffic congestion. In modern cities, traffic congestion costs the economy billions of dollars, but it is not always easy to introduce policies that alleviate congestion. For example, it is well-known that New York City has extreme traffic congestion and substantial pollution, with extremely adverse health effects. The smog caused significant damage to buildings. There have been multiple proposals over the past several decades to reduce traffic

---

[5]Manasseh, Tamar. 10/22/2017. We are Reclaiming Chicago One Corner at a Time. *New York Times*. Tamar Manasseh is President and founder of Mothers Against Senseless Killings.

congestion in Manhattan by introducing tolls and parking bans.[6] However, all such proposals, including the latest one from 2017 have been defeated by the state legislature.[7] In some cases, the proposals were defeated due to opposition from New York's parking industry,[8] and in other cases by representatives from outer boroughs whose constituents felt that congestion tolls would harm them, without compensating benefits in the form of improved public transportation. The value, in this case, is that you need placemaking and services for the development of urban spaces. This can be seen in the case of Madison with the city's commitment to bike paths, but, what about the space of multifamily buildings? New York has far more multi-family buildings than Madison and many more mid-sized family buildings. Let us consider a potential mid-sized unit: 8 to 12 families. In both cases, the development of these mid-sized units has been commonly viewed as a factor in the decline of urban neighborhoods, the increase of crime, and the reduction of services. It is not enough to have people who value a neighborhood; it is more important to have people who are willing to fight for that community. This is critical in the case of Madison, which has a disproportionate number of the low-income families when compared to the Dane County and the Wisconsin average.

The Case of Madison, Wisconsin

Over the past 30–40 years, Madison's population has grown much faster than the surrounding areas, and adding to the housing stock has been critical. In a balanced market, the vacancy rate should be around 5%. This is also known as equilibrium vacancy. As we will see later in this chapter, rental vacancy in Madison fell below 2% in 2013 and was still under 3% in the first quarter of 2017.

To meet the demand for housing from the growing number of households, Madison needs to build at least 1000 units per year. A restriction on this need is that each municipality can only develop on land that belongs to that municipality. There are also surrounding areas, such as suburbs, which have restrictions that allow them to take on developments of low-density, expensive houses, ensuring that there will not be any affordable housing development projects in their municipalities. These restrictions mean that affordable housing development in Madison is necessarily limited to the land that the city has close with access to bus routes. Some approaches to affordable housing in Midwestern municipalities have suggested that the city should not take any role in addressing the problem, leaving solutions up to negotiations between the state, the federal government, and the private market.

---

[6]See Hu, Winnie. 11/28/2017. New York's Tilt Toward Congestion Pricing Was Years in the Making. *New York Times*.

[7]See Hu, Winnie and Jesse McKinley. 4/9/2018. Congestion Pricing Plan for Manhattan Ran into Politics. Politics Won. *New York Times*.

[8]See Confessor, Nicholas. 4/7/2018. Congestion Pricing Plan Dies in Albany. *New York Times*.

Critically, the approach that considers the importance of local governance structures suggests that this is not the case. Instead, this locally rooted approach indicates that there is a distinct need, particularly for the homeless population, for rehabilitation, and that this requirement is a more robustly supplied labor market. Consider the following metaphor for the need to maintain some aspect of municipal governance: *If it were to rain gold every 2 days, we should not let the gold wash down into the drains, but instead, create a service to capture and refine the gold.* We should view all potential laborers and their family in the same fashion. This argument suggests that we should be committed to the development of 800 to 1000 new affordable housing units per year in cities with populations of roughly 250,000 and 1% population growth rates.

Currently, the City of Madison is building between 200 and 400 units per year, and therefore, the city needs to double its potential pace of affordable housing development more than to barely keep up with the demand of the natural growth of the city. The city has incrementally increased the annexation of eligible surrounding farmland to increase the available size of potential development plots. It was 60 square miles of area in 1973 and is about 76 square miles of plots now, meaning that in the past 44 years, the city has annexed about 16 square miles, or one square mile of land every 3 years.

When there are protests about the potential of the affordable housing development, the city does not have to worry about the community organizations beyond its attempt to keep the neighborhood associations content, from a policy perspective, since the city ultimately can overrule them for the sake of the need for affordable housing development.

Regarding the relationship with the developer, the city also does not have to worry as much, since they do not purchase the land, although they do have the governance over which land is developed. As discussed in Chap. 3, the state allocates the tax-credits through Wisconsin Housing and Economic Development Authority (WHEDA), and there is a scoring sheet for this platform.[9]

The City of Madison's Urban Policy and Development Initiatives

A city's Housing Initiatives Specialists might have a variety of titles. A good person to seek out for such advice would be someone with the title "Head of Real Estate" with the local municipal government. It would be ideal if this individual had some experience working with federal agencies, had an MBA, and worked closely with the development of urban policy on housing through a Housing Strategy Committee. Such a committee should be composed of Developers, Landlords, Realtors, Bankers, Funders, and members of Academia. The task of such a committee would be to

---

[9]See https://www.wheda.com/

produce research reports intended to understand the city's housing needs, as well as make recommendations to decision-makers about strategies to address such needs. A good example is the City of Madison's Biennial Housing Report, written by the city's housing initiatives specialist for the Housing Strategy Committee. The focus for their biennial report would be topics such as "Affordability and Housing." Each chapter of the report would look at what the supply is and what the demand is. The report asks: *What are other cities doing? What are best practices our municipality can learn from?* The report includes chapters on Homelessness, Low Income Rental, Market Rate Rental, Low Income Ownership, Market Rate Ownership, Senior Housing, and Student Housing. In Madison, there is a committee that follows this model and works most closely with the Community Development Authority (CDA), which owns nearly 900 units across the city.[10]

In Chap. 1, we discussed the housing affordability challenges that Madison faces, as outlined in the Biennial Housing Report. In the remainder of this chapter we discuss the policies and practices the municipal government has adopted to deal with this issue. Currently, there are substantial challenges to the development of affordable housing in the City of Madison, as well as nationwide. The rate of federal assistance is shrinking or flat. This trend is true across the board for Public Housing, Section 8, and HOME funds. Even the Community Development Block Grant (CDBG), is shrinking.[11] Section 42 funding remains relatively stable, but only half of the projects that are proposed for Section 42 are funded. Construction costs, the cost of labor, materials, and land, have been rising by about 7% annually. Some of the increased cost in materials is a result of hurricanes and weather patterns in other parts of the country where these supplies would normally come from. There is a certain amount of physical capacity to add supply to the housing market as well, as our research highlights that there is limited land in the city. Instead of simple expansion, acquiring sites, assembling property, and providing adequate onsite parking will pose a significant challenge to develop in these limited locations.

The strategy of the City of Madison for affordable housing has been multifaceted. They have created a $25 million affordable housing fund. The city can extend the tax increment generated from existing Tax Increment Districts and has thus established a special fund (Affordable Housing Fund), which is leveraged into more affordable housing that would be built otherwise. The city also actively recruits developers. They align their recruitment with federal cycles as well.

---

[10] The City of Madison reports that the Community Development Authority owned and operated 742 units of public housing for seniors and individuals with disabilities in 2017. Additionally, they owned and operated 115 units of multifamily housing, with barrier free units for disabled individuals, particularly people with special needs, the elderly and families in need. These programs are subdivided into multifamily units, run by WHEDA, Section 8 housing, funded by vouchers, and public housing, supported by HUD funds.

[11] See Center on Budget and Policy Priorities (2011, 2016). The trend has been longstanding for Section 8 vouchers. For a more contemporary discussion on the most recent federal policy see: Capps (2017).

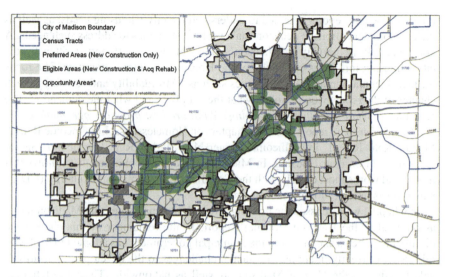

Fig. 2.1 City of Madison 2016 affordable housing targeted area map

The city's Call for Proposals goes out about 6 months before the deadline for tax credit application deadline. Within 1 or 2 months developers submit their proposals to the city. If the proposal meets the city's requirement regarding unit mix, location, and other criteria, then the city agrees to fund the project. However, they are competitive, funding only about two-thirds or less of projects, based on a feasibility analysis. If the developer can secure funding from the city, this will strengthen their Section 42 tax credit application and make it more likely the project will receive tax credits. About 3 months after the tax credit application is submitted to WHEDA, the successful applications are announced (for example, for the 2018 cycle the application deadline was in December 2017, and awards were announced in February 2018). If the developer's application is successful, the developer begins to sell their tax credits to the investor (starting in February 2018 in our previous example), a process that takes approximately 9 months. Then they receive land use approvals and a list of 40 conditions that must be met. Then, they have just 9 months to create the building, and the entire process is only 2 years long.

Since 2014, the city has maintained a map of areas that it considers most and least suitable for construction of affordable housing. Figure 2.1 shows the 2016 version of this map.

The green locations are sites that are preferred by the city, light grey sites are viewed as acceptable, and dark grey is where the city would not like any more affordable housing construction. The dark grey areas are already areas with a high density of low-income housing, and the city motivation for this coding is to attempt to avoid the process of concentrating low-income housing in certain neighborhoods, essentially. The scoring data on the map matches the Wisconsin Housing and Economic Development Authority (WHEDA) state geographic targeting. The WHEDA scoring is acceptable, although it doesn't consider student populations, which is problematic. Using this proactive approach, in the past 3 years, the City of Madison has been able to leverage $7.5 million in investment (from the Affordable Housing Fund) to support $100 million worth of affordable housing. There are a total of 462 units and a mix of 30%, 50% and 60% of AMI units.

In their review of tax credit applications, the state agency in charge of allocating the tax credits uses a point scoring system to evaluate projects (see Luque 2018). These points are distributed among different categories. For example, the WHEDA's 2017 QAP assigns a total of 284 points to the following categories (points in parentheses): lower-income areas (5), energy efficiency and sustainability (32), mixed-income incentive (12), serves large families (5), serves lowest-income residents (60), supportive housing (20), rehab/neighborhood stabilization (25), universal design (18), financial participation (25), eventual tenant ownership (3), development team (12), readiness to proceed (12), credit usage (30), and opportunity zones (25). Developers prepare their affordable housing proposals trying to score the maximum points for as many categories as possible, but sometimes financial and physical barriers prevent developers from getting high scores in some of these categories. The maximum annual credit allocation is usually either 4% or 9% of the eligible basis of a project depending on factors such as the type of affordable housing development project (e.g., rehabilitation versus new construction) and the use of tax exempt bonds.[12]

Municipal leaders have also created strategies to address the crisis of market-rate rental housing units through providing better information and communication across agencies, producing a Quarterly Housing Data Report, and aim for increasing representation by rental housing providers on city committees. They have also created a development district initiative. That initiative identifies areas in the comprehensive plan. It prioritizes neighborhood planning and the creation of zoning overlay, as well as urban design districts (assess areas that could handle 3000 units for several more years). It has created a TIF strategy, established Direct Affordable Housing Funds, and would like to put more emphasis on a Land Banking Fund. The Land Banking Fund acquires a brownfield site with contamination, as a large parcel. They buy it, clean it up and subdivide it to sell it to the market. They have a current idea to combine: City, County, Utility, and banks to be able to fund these different initiatives.

Figure 2.2 shows Madison's affordable housing targeted area map, with the locations of the actual projects completed or under construction identified. As the map shows, the city has been relatively successful in attracting buildings to its preferred locations: the majority of the projects are within the preferred (green) areas. In the cases where projects were built in areas not identified by the city, the developer has often controlled the site for years and has more or less committed to building there.

---

[12]The eligible basis of a project is the cost of acquiring an existing building if there is one (but not the cost of the land), plus construction and other construction-related costs to complete the project.

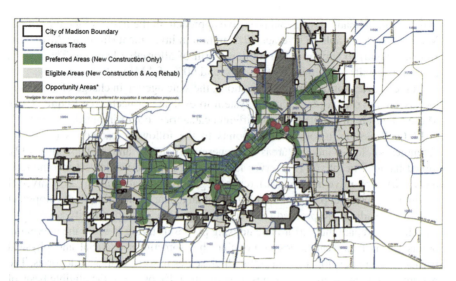

Fig. 2.2 City of Madison 2016 affordable housing targeted area map, with actual projects completed or under construction

Finally, sometimes state preference overrides city preference. For example, in a recent case on the west side of the city: there was considerable growth in low-wage jobs. But, the city didn't look at these sites as ideal because the bus doesn't run mid-day or doesn't run on Sunday. Nonetheless, the state overrode the municipality and prioritized developing the site because of the location next to employment opportunities.

In the future, the City of Madison needs merely to increase its housing options, and there are some policy change initiatives that could allow for this. First and foremost, the municipal government could allow for increased density (raise height units, smaller units). Next, they could levy more programs toward the usage of Tax Increment Financing (TIF) for affordability (currently banned to an extent). However, such a model is complicated in a university town such as Madison because affordability is based on income and income is not a reliable measure of the wealth of students, so long as they are not independent students.

In addition, in surrounding neighborhoods with middle-density housing, single-family homes could be converted into 8-unit houses. But, the cost could be up to $250,000 million to renovate such units. There are solutions that could be put forward with the introduction of a small cap TIF program. Alternatively, these units could just be demolished and middle-density construction could replace them. But then, the city would have to allow demolition which could be quite tricky in some neighborhoods.

It might also be possible to enforce housing policies for certain types of particularly vulnerable populations (single moms or post-prison population). For example, one could ask to set aside 25% of units for a vulnerable population, such as survivors of domestic abuse. But how much you could or would want to enforce these policies as a management company is a difficult question to answer. *Would you go through a referral agency? What happens if you don't meet the demand in a given number of months?* Furthermore, when one applies for tax credits, there are different (often contradictory) conditions—some ask for less money/unit—and if you meet those requirements, you will score better. Taking on more debt will score better. Serving mixed-income gets you points as well. But serving low income and serving mixed-income communities would be naturally contradictory scoring categories, for example, it would be impossible to do well on both.

Local Policy At the County Level: Initiatives and Challenges

The primary task of Dane County level governance concerning affordable housing is to assess the needs of the housing gap and enact policy to treat these needs. Housing gap is the difference between the units that are available and the units that are needed: the housing gap creates debt, overcrowded housing, and health risks. While the State of Wisconsin is declining concerning population, Dane County has the highest population growth in the state. 25% of the population growth in the state is in Dane County. There are 66,000 cost burdened (33%) of renter households. So even though a full third of renters are cost-burdened, Section 8 housing vouchers are not available to all qualified households—there is currently a 2-year wait list.

Housing need can be found in Table 6.2 of the Paulsen Report for Dane County (Paulsen 2015).[13] Locally, four public housing authorities are concerned with addressing these needs, and they are Dane County, Madison, Stoughton, and DeForest. Currently, the Dane County Housing Authority is tasked with operating over 1000 public housing units, and 3000 Section 8 vouchers, theoretically. However, declining HUD funds have led to the actual funding of only 2500 Section 8 funding vouchers out of the 3000 units, meaning the program has a shortfall of nearly 500 voucher housing units needed even wholly to house their existing families eligible for housing vouchers.

In the past, HUD had been robustly responsible for substantial Sections 202, 236, and 811—special needs funds—which went more substantially toward funding those families at the county level of governance. However, the Tax Reform Act of 1986 shifted the funds almost entirely into Section 42 LIHTC housing developments (under Section 42 of the code; see Chap. 3). For the county, this has introduced a new challenge, since Municipality levels of governance more frequently take Section 42 funding.

There are many issues and concerns for the Dane County Housing Authority that developers should keep in mind when working with them. First and foremost, competition between programs tends to increase targeted cuts for subsidies in the less successful programs. Furthermore, development costs invariably grow each

---

[13] See Paulsen (2015).

year. At the same time, the most significant level of uncertainty is in the realm of policy reforms that the county authority is subject to, but has no power to change. These guidelines are mostly established at the state, and or federal, level of governance. For example, if the corporate tax rate is cut, the fear at the county level is that tax credits will likely lose their sellable value, or that their sellable value will decrease, making tax credit projects less viable. We expand and deepen the discussion of tax credit projects in the following chapter (Chap. 3).

Concerning the county's responsibility, it is minimal in this process. However, they do provide some oversight of tax credit level projects following the pattern: LIHTC (Low Income Housing Tax Credit) investors contract their tax credits to a large corporation to transfer the ownership of the project for 15 years, through an LLC, at which point they usually sell the project to the limited partner for a nominal fee. During the first ten, they get 10 years of tax breaks. WHEDA then continues to be a supervisor, ensuring that the development follows local regulations. For the county, one problem with the tax credit program is that after 30 years, the project transfers to the market rate. So, we have housing from the 1960s through 1980s that is being converted to market rate housing.

The Dane County Housing Initiative (DCHI) is a policy, programming and education initiative that is targeted at establishing progress in the substantial need for affordable housing in the Dane County market. The organization is a public-private partnership platform, which operates resources to assist with public housing needs. They facilitate public outreach and education programs, as well as provide technical assistance, in an effort to abate the affordable housing crisis. DCHI's scope is geographical, organizational, planning and development. They foresee themselves as primarily coordinating committees, in an ideal policy world, consisting of housing stakeholders, local government staff, academics, and non-profits. Occasionally they collaborate with city officials, such as in the case of the Messner site development,[14] which is ongoing, although the Messner site is considered unique from the perspective of the county office. Typically, Housing Needs Assessments are made at the local and municipal level. The Wisconsin Department of Public Instruction (DPI), for example, keeps a list of homeless students in the public schools. School Districts also play an essential role in these assessments, since children are often at the front line of the need for services. The Homeless Services Consortium of Dane County and the City of Madison identifies and attempts to create an evaluation of risk homeless population from a county-wide perspective. Furthermore, there is a "Homeless prioritization list" and the "by name list" of the city homeless population. One issue for the DCHI committee is to consider the expansion of public transportation, the creation of new transit solutions, or the shift of transit zones, to account for the nature of the developments.

One of the critical outputs of the DCHI project thus far has been the Dane County Housing Summit (DCHS).[15] The purposes of the DCHS are education and expand

---

[14]See Mesch (2017).

[15]See the website: communityyoutreach.countyofdane.com/HousingInitiative

housing options. The outcomes from DCHS include building a network housing stakeholders and increasing understanding of issues related to housing gap. In the first year of the project, they have introduced the concept of the "Housing Gap," as well as a platform to better assess the needs of housing in Dane Country, and established programs that have built relationships with non-profits and developers. In the second year of the project, they want to focus more intently on the specific issues of the housing gap, on financing and communication strategies, on children and homelessness, as well as on planning and zoning tools. In the third year of the project, they want to focus more on the workforce of the region. The aim is to assess the housing needs of each neighborhood. They also boast an exciting new project in Sun Prairie, by Gorman & Company.

Conclusion

In this chapter, we have considered the conditions of homelessness, housing policy and urban planning. With respect to the concerns of the homeless population of midwestern cities, we at first focused predominantly on the needs of transportation and housing, although we took care to note the importance of childcare, education/skills and training, and healthcare, notably including the oftenignored categories of nutrition, mental health care, and substance abuse as other realities impacting homeless populations. We noted that it is possible for unbalanced urban economies to create new numbers of urban poor, while we also accepted that families who are low income might arrive in mid-sized cities from larger cities for a multitude of reasons, including safety and job prospects. We established the working premise that a household that commits more than 30% of their income to housing would feel financial stress, while a household that spends 50% of their income on housing costs will have economic woes. Furthermore, we noted that many stereotypes of homeless populations, such as that "the overwhelming majority have a criminal history" are not accurate based upon the available data, although the numbers are still high. We recognized that *Housing First* in these circumstances has been the working premise of the City of Madison for the past several decades, and examined the potential usefulness of very merely community based approaches that are practiced in the City of Chicago, as reported in the *New York Times*, highlighting the importance of how community building can transform even previously dangerous areas into much more livable communities. We then dove more in-depth into the local case study, considering the perspectives of local experts and local policymakers.

From the perspective of local experts and policymakers, the idea that the homeless population in Madison is arriving from outside the area seems not particularly nuanced. Instead the data seems to suggest that populations of new potential workers are coming to the city—mostly from other parts of the state of Wisconsin—and then living in unstable housing situations, only to be inevitably priced out of an incredibly unbalanced market, where an individual household would need a combined income of $60,000/year to afford $1500/month in housing costs, the rough cost of a two-bedroom apartment. To highlight the need we established: renters increased 17,000 between 2007 and 2015, with a tremendous jump in total need of more than 5000 units that the city has not met, of that total. Currently, there are also 7000–8000 non-student renters who are spending more than half of their income on rental units, creating severe individual economic stress. To begin to meet these needs, the city has targeted the poorest of the poor but also give them proper housing, such as a LEED Platinum and PassiveHouse certified development of 60 units which meets both measures of sustainable development and provides all the service needs for formerly homeless individuals who are housed in the structure. Nevertheless, the current demand for affordable housing remains enormous, with only 100 to 200 units of a needed 1500 to 2000 units being built each year. To continue to meet this need, the City of Madison will have to work with developers, CDA programs, including public housing, Section 8 housing, and WHEDA housing. Another critical policy for urban planners to consider is the Naturally Occurring Retiring Neighborhoods (NORCs) and to focus on the rehabilitation of housing in those areas, along with the building of new resources.

As we have highlighted the importance of county-level county-level policymakers in this chapter, we have also emphasized the need to understand working with standing committees, to be attuned to the potential shifting the tax burden on specific communities, particularly with relation to the property tax value of tracts that are marked for development, as well as the potential benefits of tax-credit programs for all parties involved. In the following chapters, we will devote particular attention to the additional programs that a developer can levy to develop NORCs in addition to addressing the tremendous housing needs of small to mid-sized Midwestern cities. For example, we devote particular attention to Tax Increment Financing (TIF) in Chap. 4.

References

Capps K (2017, April 11) Tracking the shadow of public housing budget cuts. City Lab. Available online at https://www.citylab.com/equity/2017/04/tracking-the-shadow-of-public-housing-budget-cuts/521778/

Center on Budget and Policy Priorities (2011, July 20) Section 8 rental assistance programs are not growing as share of HUD budget. Available online at https://www.cbpp.org/research/section-8-rental-assistance-programs-are-not-growing-as-share-of-hud-budget

Center on Budget and Policy Priorities (2016, April 12) Cuts in federal assistance have exacerbated families' struggles to afford housing. Available online at https://www.cbpp.org/research/housing/chart-book-cuts-in-federal-assistance-have-exacerbated-families-struggles-to-afford

Confessor, Nicholas (2018, April 7) Congestion pricing plan dies in Albany. New York Times

Glaeser EL (2011) Triumph of the city: how our greatest invention makes us richer, smarter, greener, healthier, and happier. Penguin Press

Hu W (2017, November 28) New York's tilt toward congestion pricing was years in the making. New York Times

Hu W, McKinley J (2018, April 9) Congestion pricing plan for Manhattan Ran into politics. Politics Won. New York Times

References

Jacobs J (1961) The death and life of Great American cities. Vintage

Luque J (2018) Assessing the role of TIF and LIHTC in an equilibrium model of affordable housing development. Reg Sci Urban Econ. Available online at https://doi.org/10.1016/j.regsciurbeco.2018.06.005. Accessed 6 July 2018

Manasseh T (2017, October 22) We are reclaiming Chicago one corner at a time. New York Times

Maslow AH (1943) A theory of human motivation. Psychol Rev 50(4):370

Mesch S (2017, February 10) County Board approves using former Messner property to create affordable housing. Wisconsin State J

Paulsen K (2015) Housing needs assessment: Dane County and municipalities. Report prepared for: Dane County Health and Human Needs Committee, Dane County Department of Human Services and Dane County Planning and Development Department

Soglin P, O'Keefe J, Wallinger S, Rhodes L (2013) Annual report on homeless persons served in Dane County. City of Madison

Whyte WH (2012) City: rediscovering the center. University of Pennsylvania Press

Chapter 3
The Low-Income Housing Tax Credit (LIHTC) Program

Abstract This chapter discusses the Low-Income Housing Tax Credits (LIHTC) program from the perspectives of the developer and the state housing authority responsible for distributing the tax credits. First, we describe the LIHTC program, how projects are financed with it, why investors are interested in LIHTC projects, and the details of the two main tax credit programs: 9% and 4% credits. Then, we discuss the perspective of the state housing authority. We consider the nature and duties of the housing authorities. We then move on to examine the mechanics of LIHTCs, how they work, and why they work for both the housing authority and the developers. We use Wisconsin's state housing authority, Wisconsin Housing and Economic Development Authority (WHEDA), as an example of how states distribute tax credits. We examine the nature of WHEDA's scoring system, what a developer can expect in this process, and how to prepare for a WHEDA application. In the third part of the chapter, we consider the perspective of the developer. We examine the process of establishing site control, the benefits of working with a small firm for these projects, the basics of the program from the perspective of a successful developer, including which tax credits they prefer to apply for and why, and some of the challenges associated with the LIHTC program.

Introduction to LIHTC

As discussed in Chap. 2, over the last three decades, federal policy has shifted from public provision of housing to subsidizing private development of affordable housing. As a result, there has been little construction of public housing over the last 25–30 years, while housing built by private developers using government subsidies has been increasing. The biggest example of this shift is the Low Income Housing Tax Credits (LIHTC) program. The Tax Reform Act (1986) established the LIHTC program under Section 42 of the Internal Revenue Code. Consequentially, it is common to refer to LIHTC as "Section 42". The goal of the program is to encourage corporate and individual investors to invest in the acquisition, development, and rehabilitation of affordable rental housing. Currently, LIHTC is the largest project-based subsidy program and has been responsible for nearly 3 million housing units built between 1987 and 2015, according to HUD. The subsidy consists of tax credits for investing in qualifying affordable housing projects. Typically, the amount of annual tax credits is the product of three factors. The first is the "eligible basis", roughly the construction cost. The second is the "applicable fraction", roughly the fraction of units that are affordable. The third is either 9% or 4%, which are the two types of tax credit programs available, with the 9% tax credit being the most competitive. This annual tax credit would be claimed for ten years. In some cases, properties located in federally designated areas or high development costs or poverty levels may be eligible for a larger allocation.[1]

Investors such as banks, insurance companies, and other large corporations, typically buy tax credits to offset their federal income tax liability. The equity raised substantially reduces the need for debt and equity financing, which can be crucial for a project's feasibility. In the case of the 9% credit, the credits pay for 90% of the eligible basis (not adjusting for time value of money, which is based on the idea that a dollar a year from now is worth less than a dollar today) or about 60–70% of total development cost. This cash infusion of more than half of the development cost reduces the required loan amount (and thus annual debt service) and substantially reduces the developer's equity contribution. However, this money comes with strings attached: the development plan must meet certain affordability conditions to qualify for tax credits. Specifically, the developer has two choices, which are known as "tests". These are the "60/40 test" and the "50/20 test". The developer absolutely must prove their plan passes one of these tests. The "60/40 test" means that tenants earning no more than 60% of the area's median income must occupy at least 40% of the units. The "50/20 test" means that tenants earning no more than 50% of the area's median income must occupy at least 20% of the units. In both cases, these units will then be subject to rent restrictions, whereby the tenants' rent, including utilities, will not exceed 30% of the area's median income. Although the developer only needs to meet one of the two tests for the project to qualify for credits, in practice most affordable housing projects the vast majority of units are affordable. The reason that developers take this approach is that it maximizes the number of tax credits their plan qualifies for, which increase as the share of affordable units goes up.

After a project is completed and put into service, the plan must continue to meet the affordability standards for 15 years, although the developer can only claim annual tax credits for ten years. In case of non-compliance, the developer might need to pay their previously claimed credits back to the IRS. State credit agencies require that the project meet the affordability requirements for an additional 15 years, for a total of the 30-year compliance period. After that, the owner has the option of converting the units into market-rate units. However, the vast majority of properties tend to remain affordable, partly because affordable housing developers tend to

---

[1] US Treasury report "Low-Income Housing Tax Credits: Affordable Housing Investment Opportunities for Banks."

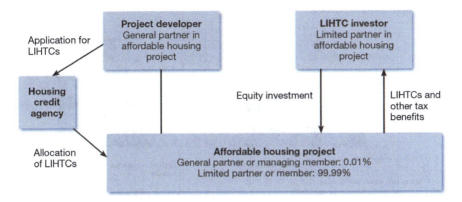

Fig. 3.1 Typical structure for direct investment in LIHTC-financed projects. Source: Office of the comptroller of the currency

specialize in this type of property, and partly because the owner will be eligible for a new round of tax credits for rehabilitation of an existing property.

LIHTC projects are usually structured as limited partnerships or limited liability corporations, with the developer as the general partner and the investor(s) as the limited partner(s). Depending on the number of investments and projects, the stakes in LIHTC projects could be structured in two ways: as a direct investment in a single partnership, or as an investment in a syndicated LIHTC-equity fund[2]. Figure 3.1 shows the first legal structure for direct investment in a LIHTC-financed project. In this arrangement, the developer (who is also the general partner of the limited partnership) applies to the state housing credit agency for credits.[3] If approved, the developer then sells the tax credits to an investor, who is the limited partner in the partnership. In exchange for this cash infusion, the investor typically receives a significant portion of the equity (99.99% in the figure). The developer retains a nominal share of equity. The cash flow return is relatively minimal over the period of investment, with the bulk of the return coming from taxes saved as well as taking advantage of depreciation deductions. After the investor receives their tax credit benefits for the entire 10-year period, it exits the partnership by selling its equity position to the developer for a nominal sum, say $1. Typically the sale occurs in years 11 to 16, after which the developer continues to own and manage the project for the remaining compliance period.

The second arrangement, which is an investment in a syndicated LIHTC-equity fund, is shown in Fig. 3.2. The idea is similar to direct investment, with two

---

[2]US Treasury report "Low-Income Housing Tax Credits: Affordable Housing Investment Opportunities for Banks."

[3]State housing credit agencies are also known as state housing authorities. Agencies' names vary widely by individual state, including authority, corporation, association, and others. The U.S. Department of Housing and Urban Development refers to state housing authorities as "LIHTC-allocating agencies".

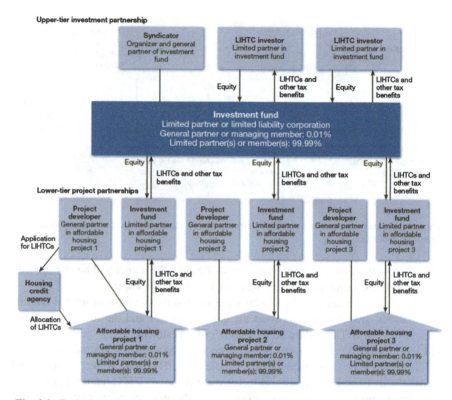

Fig. 3.2 Typical structure for investment in a syndicated LIHTC-financed equity fund. Source: Office of the Comptroller of the Currency

differences. First, syndication involves creating a fund of multiple affordable housing projects. Second, this fund is generated by a syndicator, who brings developers and investors together. An additional difference is that syndication allows participation for smaller investors because it requires a lower minimum investment than a direct investment in an individual development project.[4]

As mentioned briefly above, there are two types of credits: 9% credit and 4% credit. The 9% credit is available for newly constructed buildings or substantial rehabilitation of existing buildings unless the construction is financed with tax-exempt bonds. The annual credit can be up to 9% of the "eligible basis", which includes most hard costs (such as construction cost), and most depreciable soft costs. The most substantial expense that is excluded from the eligible basis is the land cost. The 9% credit can be claimed annually for ten years, for a total of 90% of the eligible basis. The project can obtain the maximum of 9% tax credit if all the

---

[4]US Treasury report "Low-Income Housing Tax Credits: Affordable Housing Investment Opportunities for Banks."

The Two Types of LIHTCs		
LIHTC type	9% (Competitive)	4% (Non-competitive)
Amount	Credit for 9% of cost per year for 10 years	Credit for 4% of cost per year for 10 years
Allocation	Based on state population, about $2.35 per resident for 2016	Tied to state's tax-exempt bond volume cap
Cycle	One allocation cycle each year	Year-round allocation cycle
Demand	High	Lower

Fig. 3.3 Summary of the 9% and 4% LIHTC programs

units are affordable; the credit would decrease as the share of market-rate units increases.

Due to its attractiveness to developers, the demand for 9% credits exceeds the funds available. Each state's cap for credits is calculated as a fixed dollar amount per resident times the state's population. For example, the State of Wisconsin had approximately $13.6 million available for the 2017 cycle. Each state allocates its 9% credits in a competitive process, and in any given year the amount of credits requested in all applications may be two to four times the amount available. In some high demand development areas, such as large metropolitan like Chicago, demand can be as high as 9:1.

The less attractive option from the developers' point of view is the 4% tax credit, which can be claimed if 50% or more of the project is financed with tax-exempt private activity bonds. The advantage of the 4% tax credits is that they are not competitive, and the developer can claim them without having to obtain a credit allocation from the state agencies. On the other hand, the 4% tax credit contributes a much smaller portion of the development costs. This forces the developers to find additional sources of financing, and in practice, 4% tax credits are combined with other federal programs, such as Home Investment Partnership Program (HOME), the Federal Home Loan Bank Affordable Housing Program, and the Community Development Block Grant Program.[5] In addition to these federal programs, developers may need to rely on state agency loans and private foundation grants. Figure 3.3 below summarizes the fundamental differences between the 9% and 4% tax credit programs.

How the LIHTC Program Is Administered at the State Level

When the LIHTC program was first created in 1986, each state received a fixed allocation of $1.25 per resident. This amount was increased several times and was set at $1.75 per resident in 2002.[6] Starting in 2003, the allocation is tied to inflation. As a

---

[5]US Treasury report "Low-Income Housing Tax Credits: Affordable Housing Investment Opportunities for Banks."

[6]Novogradac and Company.

result, in 2016 each state received the greater of $2.35 per resident or the state minimum of $2.69 million. States with smaller populations like Delaware, Montana, South Dakota, and North Dakota all received the state minimums for the 2016 allocation cycle, while California and Texas received $92 million and $63.4 million, respectively. For the purposes of program effectiveness, it should be noted that a larger allocation does not necessarily translate into the creation of more affordable housing units. For example, for the 19-year period between 1987 and 2005, California built 115,478 units using a total allocation of $932 million. During the same period, Texas built more units (159,296) with a little over half the allocation ($500 million).[7] This reflects the large differences in land and house prices in the two states. Currently, the total allocation for all 50 states and Washington, DC is almost $8 billion.[8]

At the federal level, the Internal Revenue Service allocates federal tax credits to each state's housing authority. As we mentioned above, the demand for the 9% tax credit tends to exceed the funds available. As a result, state housing authorities then award the credits to individual projects based on their points-based selection criteria. According to federal law, each state housing credit agency must have a Qualified Allocation Plan (QAP), which establishes the state's criteria and priorities for awarding 9% tax credits. The QAP requires approval from the housing authority board, as well as from the governor. Based on the Internal Revenue Code, Section 42 (m)(1)(C), at a minimum, the state agencies' criteria must include: location, housing needs, public housing waiting lists, individuals with children, special needs populations, whether a project includes the use of existing housing as part of the community revitalization plan, project sponsor characteristics, and projects intended for eventual tenant ownership. However, individual state agencies may and do go beyond these minimum criteria, and develop more specific criteria according to their priorities. For example, the federal law mandates that the project meet either the 40/60 test *or* the 20/50 test, meaning it is possible for a project to qualify for some tax credits with only 20% of its units being affordable. However, most state housing authorities encourage to offer more than this minimum number, as well as provide units for the lowest-income tenants. Because the amount of tax credits is proportional to the share of affordable units, most projects end up having only affordable units, as well as reserving some units for renters with incomes less than half of area median income.[9]

---

[7]Glaeser and Gyuorko (2008) and Danter Company (2006).
[8]U.S. Department of Housing and Urban Development.
[9]Office of the Comptroller of the Currency.

WHEDA: How Wisconsin Does LIHTC

As we mentioned earlier, at the state level the LIHTC program is administered by each state's respective housing authority. Wisconsin's state housing authority, Wisconsin Housing and Economic Development Authority (WHEDA), was created in 1972 by state statute with a mission to "to stimulate the state's economy and improve the quality of life for Wisconsin residents by providing affordable housing and business financing products." Currently, WHEDA has about $2.2 billion in assets. WHEDA's activities can be described as a long-term, public-private partnership, which emphasizes collaboration between the public and private sectors of the market.

Just like every other state's housing authority, WHEDA operates two types of tax credits, a 4% and a 9% tax credit. The state's allocation of 9% tax credit for 2016 was $13.6 million. The 4% is tied to state's tax-exempt bond volume cap. Hence, the 4% credit is not competitive. However, as an applicant, the developer wants the 9% credit, as that could cover close to 90% of the costs in the relevant sector of the budget, substantially reducing the need for other sources of funds.

Because states can have different needs concerning affordable housing, individual states' criteria for awarding tax credits often vary. Most states' criteria include questions like:

What is the likelihood of receiving an award from other sources?
    Are rents reasonable?
    Is the project meet the 40/60 or 20/50 test?
    Are expected rents below the limits?
    Does the project have room to increase the rent?
    Does the project meet minimum design requirements?
    Is there evidence of demand for units in the current market conditions?

To answer these questions satisfactorily, the developer needs to submit a market study completed for the project. In Wisconsin, proposed projects meeting the thresholds are scored against other similar applications in their set-aside category: non-profit, supportive housing, rural, preservation, general. The reason for this is that similar projects can compete against a similar plan. The applications are then scored. There is also bonus scoring in the process for: serving low income; energy efficiency, and sustainability; credit usage; opportunity zones; financial participation[10]. In Chap. 2, we discussed the various categories used by WHEDA. Figure 3.4 shows the summary of WHEDA's points-based scoring system for the 2017 cycle.

Currently, WHEDA manages approximately $350 million in LIHTC. As the developer looks at these particular programs, they have to select how much of the development will be represented by the housing for which parts of the housing market, as per their share of the County Median Income (CMI). There are requirements for the programs. The essential conditions are the 20/50 and 40/60 rules:

---

[10]Credit usage and financial involvement *ask for evidence of* leverage funding from other sources for the deal.

	Maximum Points
1. Lower-Income Areas	5
2. Energy Efficiency and Sustainability	32
3. Mixed-Income Incentive	12
4. Serves Large Families	5
5. Serves Lowest-Income Residents	60
6. Supportive Housing	20
7. Rehab/Neighborhood Stabilization	25
8. Universal Design	18
9. Financial Participation	25
10. Eventual Tenant Ownership	3
11. Development Team	12
12. Readiness to Proceed	12
13. Credit Usage	30
14. Opportunity Zones	25
Total	284

Fig. 3.4. WHEDA's scoring system for the 2017 Low Income Housing Tax Credit Program

developments must offer a choice of 20% percent of their units targeted toward families and individuals at 50% of CMI, or 40% at/below 60% CMI. But the economics of the project usually dictates the optimal mix of affordable and market rent units. For example, they might offer 50% of their units to 20–30% of CMI, 25% of their units to those at 60% CMI, and another 25% at market rate to offset the costs in the equation.

Once the project is completed, the state housing authority is responsible for monitoring, to make sure that the units remain affordable for the entire 30-year compliance period. Furthermore, if the original developer sells the property, this does not free up the agreement from the perspective of the new owner. This agreement, called a LURA, is a long-term bound contract. It cannot be extinguished, even if there is a desire by all parties involved. For the 30-year compliance period, residents have to show that they are income eligible. The units are checked every three years. Much of the information is submitted electronically. One only must prove income when they move in. Therefore, if one determines they meet the income requirements initially, they can stay if they want; at least until 140% of CMI. So, if they increase their income to 62% of CMI, it is not a problem. The question of quality control is essential. Little flairs such as awnings or counter construction in individual units can vary highly to make the unit more affordable.

The cost of compliance is an essential operating expense to consider. It may seem small, but it is not negligible. It costs more to operate $20–25/month of additional management costs per individual. Operating costs are about $400 to $475 per month to run a unit. The market study costs are more substantial: five to six thousand dollars. An appraisal is another $2000–3000, an option on the site requires at

$8000–10,000, and the application fee to WHEDA is another $2000. Hence, the developer can expect to input at least $30,000 into a project.

In addition to Tax Credits, WHEDA covers some financing in the form of loans. There is not a question about the type of these loans, although there have been some more public questions about the nature of these programs. The current board tends to hold the position that WHEDA loans should be exclusively reserved for the debt that other lenders won't or don't cover. At the same time, many investors in affordable housing projects also want to be the lender on the project. It would not be uncommon to find that the lender is technically another company, although they might be a distant relative, or even a not too distant relative, in the same corporate family. Probably in a third to a half of deals investors and lenders are different branches of the same income structure. The risk is not high, because the demand for 30–40% CMI units is high.

WHEDA Scoring and LIHTC Applications

WHEDA scoring begins with the sites that are identified by county authorities in the State of Wisconsin. In the contemporary model of WHEDA scoring, there are 31 sites. WHEDA takes the primary role in the community as a tax credit manager, a position that they have filled since 1992. They do both policy and community outreach, along with supervising underwriters. They complete about 30 to 35 tax credit deals per year, and also work with financing for about 30 to 35 transactions per year, meaning that they are directly involved with establishing 60 to 70 development projects per year. They underwrite the tax credits each year based on a Request for Proposals (RFP). They receive about 50 applications for each cycle. Because there are only a limited number of funds for tax credits per period, a useful rubric would be to assume that only half of these proposals are accepted. Approved plans must meet a requirement of 14 individual criteria that are set by the authority of the WHEDA board.

In the past, the typical cycle for applications for Tax Credits from WHEDA began in early March. The applications would start to be prepped by this, but they would probably begin the process of conducting their research and even establishing site control a bit earlier. The awards for the previous cycle were released on May 15, 2017. Then, the development would have ten weeks to do site reviews, clear their plans with various authorities, and establish how they plan to use the tax credits that they were awarded. However, the problem with this particular cycle was that this left some developers to face their construction projects during the winter. Since winter is not an ideal time to be working on construction in Wisconsin, for the coming cycle, WHEDA adjusted the date. For the coming cycle, December 8, 2017, has been set to clear up the timeline for construction to begin in the spring because the time from the grant of the award to close can be about six months for the developer. Based on the current cycle, a developer should hope that the awards will be set by March 1, 2018. If they receive good news, they will be tasked with the project of finding an investor and securing their debt provider, a process that could take about four to six months, depending on the nature of the process. Most projects must secure two to three investors, such that they build relationships with them to work with them regularly. They then plan to finish in July and September. The months of July and September are when all the progress on the research end of the development begins to come to fruition. Financials and budgets are submitted, applications are reviewed to ensure that they are still reasonable. WHEDA also does another round of checking to make sure that the developer will provide the services that they say that they will provide, that they are committed to feasibility and staying true to the plan. If there are any issues, such as a $450,000 hole in the budget, they then recommend adjustments or agree on adjustments. Adjustments can be made if the project is not too far over budget. For example, a $2 million over expenditure would be viewed as unreasonable.

Preparing for the WHEDA Application: Research

The application process for WHEDA requires a substantial amount of research. The developer needs at least site control, an option to buy, or an opportunity to purchase the site. They also require evidence that there is a market for an affordable housing development on the site, conducted by a third party approved research firm. But this business should be able to estimate such variables as what the vacancy will be, what the reasonable rents will be, how many income-qualified households are required, what the income of the qualified families should be, what the area scoring for access to amenities is, what the performance of other TIF properties in the vicinity of the city are (see Chap. 4), and who the major employers in the region are, and what the major market activities in keeping employers and laying employees off are. The developer should be able to develop a reliable portfolio that assesses the financial feasibility of the project. The portfolio includes the operating assumptions, the debt coverage ratio, how much they are budgeting—and—if it is enough to attract an investor to the project; along with how they propose to mount funds toward any subordinate debt, through equity, HOME funds, and city subsidies (or a combination of the five).

How Developers Can Use LIHTC in Practice

It is critical to understand that the very definition of *what is affordable* has changed since the LIHTC program was created three decades ago. Additionally, "affordability" has different meanings for each urban context. Two communities within the same municipal area, or greater metro area, could appear similar from the distance of a federal survey. However, from the perspective of an urban developer, they could just as well be on two different planets. In a single county with an 18-mile radius,

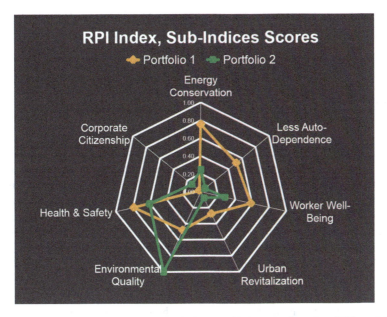

Fig. 3.5 An application of James Graaskamp's Responsible Property Investing (RPI) model

there can be three to five different development worlds entirely. Part of the theoretical challenge is understanding the zoning regulations of each area, which limit the type of federal assistance a developer might be able to use. Hence, understanding zoning regulations is the key that unlocks the potential of a development community. On the ground, the developer is now the mechanic of the new development, not the king. The need for them to be in close contact with the community has increased over the course of the last several decades. A new set of questions must come with this approach to development.

> What about amenities?
> What will it do for our taxes?
> What will it do for our schools?
> What is it going to do to my community?
> What is it going to do for my planet?

These were all questions James Graaskamp asked in the 1960s, but they are considered standard practice today. He advocated evaluating investment properties and portfolios using the Responsible Property Investment (RPI) index, which essentially analyzes real estate on six sustainability criteria. Figure 3.5 shows Graaskamp's Responsible Property Investing (RPI) model applied to two different portfolios. In this example, Portfolio 1 scores higher on all dimensions, except corporate citizenship and environmental quality.

Developers regularly must have the question "*What is the goal here?*" in mind. Naturally, the individual developer seeks cash flow, and LIHTC programs assist with that significantly. But this goal cannot be achieved through community relationships, and community-based issues are addressed through the establishment of site control by the developer.

Establishing Site Control

Madison, Wisconsin is home to about 250,000 people, who live in one of the city's 136 neighborhoods. Most neighborhoods have organized themselves into neighborhood associations, with websites and list-serves, chair people and alderpeople. A neighborhood might have 1000 households, but only 30 may show up in a meeting (for example, about a proposed development project), and ten may actively participate in a discussion. Hence, the developer has to find the "swing vote"—some who do not understand, and those who understand a lot—folks in the middle who might not say much, but they may vote. These are the critical individuals to convince at the neighborhood level. The developer has to explain their ideas in straightforward terms. Fortunately for developers in the case of Madison, a neighborhood association can cast a no vote on a project, or a vote that is not close, and they might still not entirely halt the development. In these cases, however, the alderperson may be in a position to add new conditions (such as eight new building conditions for the development, for example) in exchange for an override of the vote. Important factors to consider are that neighborhoods tend to look more favorably on the proposal to develop or rehab "eyesore properties". Such "eyesore property buys"—which could also eliminate high rate of police calls—are looked upon favorably by the city. Still, the public looks less favorably upon such projects sometimes, because they would rather have problems that are familiar, rather than potential problems that they cannot predict or cannot understand. Demolition and reconstruction projects, hence, become very difficult in Madison, even in circumstances when a structure might well be considered unlivable by potential residents. Furthermore, residents often worry about the potential of crime in new developments in their communities. Hence, it is not unreasonable to expect to invest in crime prevention through environmental design and additional lighting, as well as for the developer to have to plan to think about where the laundry location is. *Is it in a well-lit area? Or, is it exposed but poorly lit?* The developer, in communication with the property manager, also has to think about particular dynamics of the neighborhood that might be seemingly out of their control. For example, they have to worry about the visitor and guest policies. They have to worry about the potential family size of units. They also will have to be aware of the possible stereotypes that they might be battling against, whether racial or otherwise, in the process of proposing their new development. Of course, landlords and developers represent different stages in the affordable housing development process, and they are normally positions that are occupied by different companies, but neighborhood associations would also like to be able to hold the developer accountable, along with the property owner, and the property manager, long-term. In this scenario, building inspectors have an incredible amount of power, and they can strain the relationship between the developer, the property manager, and the neighborhood association.

Housing Authorities, such as the Wisconsin Housing and Economic Development Authority (WHEDA), often get pressed hard by neighborhood associations to become more accountable for the developments that they are proposing. At this point, developers have the impression that WHEDA would much rather take a development proposal in a middle-class neighborhood than a low-income neighborhood. In this context, it is appropriate to ask: *Are partnerships with non-profits, such as Porchlight, viewed favorably?* It took the City of Madison and Dane County years to locate sites for homeless housing in the city because even low-income residents refused housing developments for homeless populations. The problem was that the city was pushing to do something about the issue, but, according to some perspectives, those communities most familiar with the potential issues associated with homelessness were, ironically, the least sympathetic to the situation. Meanwhile, even idealistic middle and high-income residents were completely resistant to the idea of changing the structure of their neighborhoods.

Theoretically, the cost of affordable housing is covered by the rent. However, it is rarely the case that rents will cover the costs of the units. Furthermore, if lenders and investors must create new services in an area, they will have to create newly onerous terms in place, so that they have the capital to cover the costs of the assets. Contrast this situation with one where the community already has the services. Then the operating costs would be low, and the cash would simply flow, theoretically. Nevertheless, the neighborhood will want to see something long-term, and yet the community will not want to enter more than a two to three-year contract, while the developer will be responsible for contracts lasting up to thirty years. Given these constraints: *How should one go to the community to sell the idea?*

A developer needs to be forward. We need to educate students and potential developers as to who they need to talk to in the communities to get their ideas approved. They need to get at least the service providers excited. The developer needs to get multiple constituencies with conflicting agendas to compromise, almost like "herding cats across a football field." "They have to sell tuna " to the cats, and they may learn that a given herd of cats might not want tuna at all, but instead, "they might want tacos."[11]

The main steps to the development model for an affordable housing unit begin with the property. First, the site must be vacant, so that the land value of the lot is comparatively attractive to a developer. The essential questions then become:

Why is it vacant?
    Why are you going to buy it?
    What is the history of the site?
    Do you need to be aware of any environmental factors?
    What is the potential value of developing the property?

---

[11] 10/26/2017. Interview with development expert.

Most of the research takes place at this stage. It could take a year or longer. The research that is conducted rapidly probably will not be thorough. It may be best to take several in-depth surveys of the history of a site to get a real sense of the history of that site. Research is not a rapid process. After the research phase is completed, however, it is best to attempt to put the site under contract. This is the second stage and should be done relatively quietly. Begin to talk about the site while it is under contract, but only slowly generate interest. If the site becomes untenable at this stage, it is imperative to walk away before getting wedded to it. However, if it continues to show potential, and site control could be established, the developer moves onto the next stage of the development process: buying the property. For affordable housing, it is essential to be ahead of the market to get the best price on the property. The property just must be purchased before it is listed. Purchasing a listed property will not grant the developer yields on the value of the land, and, furthermore, will attract much more attention to the site. Next, it is essential to develop the affordable housing units by associated risk groups, by preparing for the low-risk populations first, then the mid-risk (single parent families) populations second, ensuring that there will be enough padding in the development to cover the additional risk associated with the affordable housing for special needs populations.

Benefits of a Small Firm

There are a few examples of what a small independent firm of a single individual, staffed by a few close associates can achieve in a relatively mid-sized affordable housing market. First and foremost, the case of Firm D is important to consider because they don't work with private lenders. Second, they work closely with the housing authority and have done so for years. Furthermore, they have existing housing that they use to levy against the risk associated with newer developments. Hence, the firm can take on a bit more additional risk than a new firm would be able to handle. For years they have been able to address their projects very often as urban renewal projects, where they are essentially rehabilitating property lots by tearing down the old construction and building new construction on the property to get the place fixed up. Firm D, like many small firms in the affordable housing development world, prefers very low-risk projects, and their long-standing partnership with the housing authority allows them to put up very little by terms of guarantees on their development projects. The housing authority essentially puts up all of the guarantees. The time on the firms' front end in terms of investment is mostly volunteer time if the tax credits are not won. If they are won, however, this is when the firm profits. They often are willing to enter into four-year contracts, which would be viewed as too long for the for-profit developer industry. They also can, because they are a smaller firm, work more closely with the alder-people, to ensure a smoother relationship with the neighborhood associations. They have good relationships with the HUD and WHEDA (National/Federal & State/Local) offices that provide their tax credits, and their standing relationship eases the flow of communication.

Like other industries, the development industry is always changing. But there are specificities to the change. Some details make each housing generation different. For example, as the millennial generation has entered the market rate housing market, they have proven that their needs for housing are substantially different from the generation that passed before them. Their demands for transportation are entirely different. They are much more likely to desire green housing, and they are far more likely to want to live in a more walkable area. At the current moment, their needs are relatively similar in these categories regardless of income level, although, as with other populations, affordable housing is considered the most needed. This is because affordable housing is just the most necessary category of housing in the market, regardless of the age of the population of the individuals who would aim to live in the housing. The difficulty becomes what the definition of affordable housing is for the broader community. From the Village of DeForest (population 8500) to downtown to other areas of the City of Madison, the definition of affordable varies considerably. Small development firms tend to prefer to develop in smaller feeling communities, partially because the same market principles apply in both small and large markets. Therefore, a small team gains experience in a smaller market, where there are fewer decisionmakers, and less legwork. Once they gain experience, they will be more likely to succeed in larger markets, since, again, the same principles apply.

The number one question of a developer is the question of how to stay afloat in a competitive market, or, in other words: *Where is the money going to come from?* In the affordable housing market, it is natural to assume that much of the income from properties will come from the rents of those properties. This is because if you are a developer and you build a property, you will expect to rent out the units of that property at a monthly rate, less the operating costs of the property, debt that needs to be paid, the taxes, and the vacancy rate. Using the *Front Door* model described in detail in Part 2 of this book, the developer can estimate the rent per square foot required to make the project feasible. With a market-rate unit, typically around 5% of the rent goes towards replacement reserves and return to equity investors, 33% goes to operating costs, 10% goes to property taxes, and a total of 52% goes to debt service. These shares are shown in Fig. 3.6.

To give an example of a market rate building square footage rent in the downtown area, consider "Ovation 309", one of the large housing developments in downtown Madison, with a $2 market price per square foot. Suppose this was affordable housing. The developer would need to trim the cost down to about $1/sq. foot, or maybe less. *How is it possible to do this?* One common misconception is that affordable units cost less to build, since they, hypothetically, use cheaper materials, contain fewer appliances, and so on. In fact, the materials used to build affordable units are virtually indistinguishable from market units and thus have the same construction costs. In one comparative case, supported by the Housing Authority in Oshkosh, Wisconsin, there was no debt in the structure. If this were Ovation, that would drop the rental cost of a $2000/month unit to just over $1000/month. By eliminating the debt services from the equation, a nice market-rate development, becomes much more affordable. This means that with the model of a financial

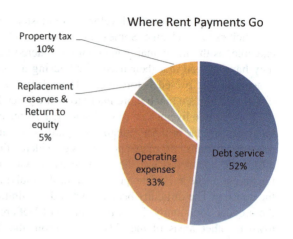

Fig. 3.6 Typical shares of the four most substantial uses of rental revenue in a multifamily property

structure being proposed, the affordability of the housing development is contained within the financial model, and not pushed onto the cost of the construction. This means that a much more high-quality structure can be built, simply by proper financing.

Site Control and Zoning: Challenges for the Developer

The greatest initial challenge for the developer in Madison is the cost of establishing site control. Land prices are high in Madison—so that this presents a problem to the developer, particularly those working in affordable housing development. Cities have seen a lot of market rate construction, but affordable housing is not financially feasible without some sort of subsidy. Most importantly here is that rents on a 30% CMI don't cover their debts, let alone their services. Addressing the community concerns is also tough. Affordable housing has to look the same as market rate housing. *How do you construct the development? Will this last for 20–30 years and serve as many people as possible?*

Cities want the material to be long-lasting, and the cost to be affordable. This puts the developer in a form of mathematical bind. Tax credits are a means of stabilizing the cost and risk for the developer, which displaces possible investment gains or losses. Furthermore, they are considered a stable investment for large corporations, which means that the use of them to fund the project is likely going to remain. The corporate pressure to keep the tax credit program balances the policy world, where tax credits are more widely approved of. Bonds, however, are considered a shakier investment, although they are stable at the moment. The question facing the bond market is one of a decline in the corporate rates. If the corporate rate for bonds drops, it is not likely that they will be as stable. Other important investment rates for the developer to consider would be depreciation rates for tax credits. If the rate of sale for the tax credit depreciates, down from approximately 92 cents on the dollar at the moment, AHP, state and federal HOME dollars, CDBG and other low-interest lending programs will become more important. Also, in a changing market, there will always be one variable that simply has to give. *In the current scenario, what is most likely to give?* Cities are not wont to accept a different quality of construction, but frequently they do. For example, they take siding instead of brick for exterior walls or consider changing parking arrangements. In that changing market, developers will not necessarily be making a 12% fee. One possible way forward, to ensure that developers still earn their same fee comparable to the value of the property, is to support more mixed-income projects and support the rates of affordable housing. Developers will have to consider what works best in a mixed-income development. If the development is mixed income, at the moment, the suggestion is that there is a 15 to 20% cap for the balance of being affordable.

Zoning is complicated—which means that developers have to spend a certain amount of time with given elected officials (have heard complaints from teachers that affordable housing makes their jobs more difficult). There are also many market and policy questions that could impact these programs shortly. For example, another way to think about the sell is "Workforce Housing." There is now a question before Congress about whether or not they will change Low-income housing to "affordable housing"? This will likely also impact the guidelines of the LIHTC or TIF programs, as we discuss in the following chapter.

References

Danter Company (2006) Detailed allocations with estimated populations. http://www.danter.com/taxcredit/allocpop.htm

Glaeser EL, Gyourko JE (2008) Rethinking federal housing policy: how to make housing plentiful and affordable. AEI Press, Washington, DC

Treasury U.S. (2014) Low-income housing tax credits: affordable housing investment opportunities for banks. Community Development Insights

U.S. Department of Housing and Urban Development (2007) Fair market rent: overview

Chapter 4
The Tax Increment Financing (TIF) Program

Abstract This chapter focuses on tax increment financing (TIF)—a powerful and favorite economic development tool. After a brief description of the program, we examine both the upsides and the downsides to the TIF program. We then continue to our primary objective—explaining how TIF works in practice, including how tax increment districts (TIDs) are created, and the process of reviewing applications. We will then look at TIF from the developers' and policymakers' perspectives.

Introduction to TIF

Tax increment financing, or TIF, enables municipalities to finance developments that, in theory, bring better infrastructure, more jobs, increased tax revenue, and other benefits to a city or district. TIF monies are given to projects that will take place in a tax increment district or TID. TIF is the most commonly utilized public tool in local economic development, and this chapter goes into some reasons why. If a city wants to increase investment in its infrastructure and services, leading to better schools, roads, and other necessities, it usually needs to increase tax revenues. Increasing tax revenue is generally done by increasing their tax basis (growing the number of taxpayers, and through property and sales taxes, although some municipalities also can charge income taxes). TIF is one way that cities can encourage growth and increase their tax revenue as well as improve quality of life for area residents. Nonetheless, cities vary in the way they collect and spend tax revenue.

Because municipal governments are highly fragmented in the U.S., strategies, and policies often differ significantly, even among cities of similar sizes with similar demographics and related industries supporting their existence. This individualized structure of local government in the U.S. makes standardization almost impossible, and very few policy tools exist that can be used across the country at the municipal level. TIF is a unique instrument in the world of local politics and can credit much of its success to how quickly it can be customized to each locality.

TIF in the United States

Tax increment financing was first adopted in California in 1952 and was initially a way of contributing local matching funds for federal subsidies. It became more and more popular in the 1970s and 1980s when federal and state grants and federal tax subsidies for economic development were gradually reduced.[1] TIF was politically more acceptable than other economic development schemes because it required no new taxes.[2] TIF remains popular across the United States for this very reason, because there is no increased tax burden on local communities—TIF proceeds are "drawn entirely from higher property taxes assessed upon future owners of property within redevelopment area boundaries."[3] Today 49 states and Washington, DC allow TIF in some form. Arizona is the only state that does not allow TIF financing in any way.

While laws governing TIF (and even its name) vary by state, most states have similar requirements for the creation of tax increment districts and for funding economic development through tax increment financing. Designating an area as a TIF district usually requires it to be "blighted" or "underdeveloped". Currently, enabling legislation in 32 states requires the finding of blight for the creation of a TIF district.[4] However, each state defines blight differently, and the term is used rather loosely. Also, most states require that a potential TIF district pass a "but for" test, which is designed to ensure that public subsidies are not used unnecessarily. This test states that "but for" the TIF funding, development would not occur at the proposed level, within the same period, or with the same level of value. In practice, both the blight requirement and the "but for" tests are low bars to clear, and they do "little to restrict the location of TIF districts."[5] Furthermore, TIF is currently the main, and in some cases the only tool, of financing local economic development in the United States.

As outlined above, the primary goal of TIF is to promote (local) economic development or redevelopment that would not otherwise occur. Within this general framework, states have prioritized some land uses or goals that can be financed using this tool. Thus, local governance structures often create TIF districts for removing blight, rehabilitation/reconstruction of existing buildings, developing industrial, retail, and mixed-use projects, environmental cleanup, and most importantly for this book, for housing, including affordable housing. As an example, Fig. 4.1 below shows the breakdown of the TID districts in Wisconsin in 2017. In this case, housing would mostly be a part of mixed-use districts.

State statutes also vary regarding the type of tax increment revenue that can be captured, which typically depends on the land use proposed with the TID. All states

---

[1] Dye and Merriman (2006).
[2] Lefcoe and Swenson (2014).
[3] Lefcoe and Swenson (2014).
[4] Council of Development Finance Agencies (2015).
[5] Dye and Merriman (2006).

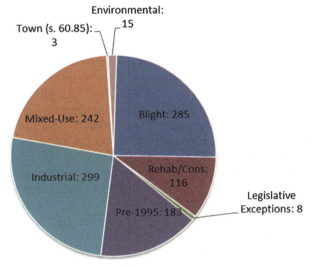

Fig. 4.1 An analysis of tax increment districts by type in Wisconsin. Source: Ehlers

allow for obtaining the property tax increment; some also allow for obtaining the increments in sales tax (for retail TIDs), payments in lieu of taxes (PILOT), and other taxes. The maximum life of TIDs varies by state and by type, and can be as short as 10 years and as long as 50 years. Some states, (e.g., AR, FL, and WI) also allow extensions to the original maximum life. Since the tax increment would go towards financing the project, the life of the TID is essential both for the viability of the project. At the same time, longer life of a TID means that the local governments are unable to collect the higher tax revenue for a longer time.

Criticisms of the TIF Mechanism

Before we get to how TIF can be used to incentivize construction of affordable housing, we need to address some of the criticisms of this financing tool. Opponents of TIF argue that it fails to achieve its stated goals, and the rules regarding the adoption of TIDs hurt some local jurisdictions. In this section, we outline some of the standard arguments against TIF and cite some evidence that backs up those claims.

Since the stated goal of TIF is to promote economic development by funding project that would not otherwise occur, it is natural to ask the question: *Does creating a TID, in fact, support economic growth?* If that were the case, property values should rise much faster in cities with TIDs than in cities without them. Evidence suggests that this is hardly the case. A 2006 study compared the changes in property values (technically, equalized assessed value—EAV) in Illinois municipalities with and without TIDs. Their results suggest that "the non-TIF areas of municipalities that use TIF grow no more rapidly, and perhaps more slowly than similar municipalities that do not use TIF."[6] The authors further considered the effects of land uses within TIDs and found that industrial TIDs did not reduce property values in the non-TID areas of the municipality. In contrast, commercial (especially retail) TIDs tended to reduce commercial property value in non-TID parts of the same town.

The likely reason that commercial (and especially retail) TIDs fail to bring long-term economic growth is that they encourage development in one part of municipality at the expense of development that would occur in other parts of the city, a process that can be called "cannibalization". There is ample evidence that new development increases the supply of space, but does not increase long-term demand.[7] So in effect, TIDs often end up shifting existing demand from one area to another. In fact, things can turn out even worse. As cities compete to attract new firms with subsidies and tax breaks, they tend to out-spend each other to attract retailers that produce less than expected sales and property taxes, ultimately reducing their tax bases significantly.[8]

Another, and possibly the most substantial, criticism of the TIF scheme is the risk-reward imbalance for the various taxing entities. In most states, the decision to designate a certain area as a TIF district is made by the municipality. Although other taxing entities are consulted in some cases, in practice the municipality is the effective decision maker. However, the TID is part of the tax base for the school district, community college district, and other taxing entities, in addition to the municipality (which may receive a minor portion of total tax revenue). The initial TIF funding amount is based on the future tax increments of *all* taxing entities combined. Therefore, by designating an area a TID, the municipality can potentially receive a huge payoff for a relatively small risk.

To illustrate, suppose the municipality receives one-fifth of the tax revenue, with the remaining four-fifths going to all other entities. In this scenario, for every 20 cents of future tax revenue the municipality gives up, the other entities effectively contribute 80 cents. So the municipality may be tempted to "capture" the growth that would have occurred even without the TID—to collect the property taxes that would have gone to the other entities. Of course, this would not be a problem if the development would not have occurred without the TIF. However, as we pointed out earlier, the "but for" test is a mere formality in most states and cities.

---

[6]Dye and Merriman (2006).

[7]Ingraham et al. (2005).

[8]Cassell and Turner (2010). See also Luque (2018) for a model of competition among TIF jurisdictions for equity investments. [Ref: Luque, J. (2018), "Assessing the role of TIF and LIHTC in an equilibrium model of affordable housing development", mimeo].

Creation of Tax Increment Districts

TIF starts with the creation of tax increment districts (or TIDs) in a city. These are sites or neighborhoods that are designated with a specific development need or urban blight and ready for renewal. The first word of TIF is" tax", and everything that occurs with a TIF project will always come back to taxation policy. This starts at the very beginning of a TIF project. In some states, including Wisconsin, all of the overlapping local government that share in the tax receipts must agree before approving and offering TIF funds to a developer. These local governments include the municipality itself, county, township, school district, community college district, library district, and many other special districts. Because TIF will limit the tax revenue received by these governments, it is imperative that all of them understand the financial impact of offering TIF to a developer, and have an opportunity to veto a project that they think will not adequately improve the TID. These tax recipients, and occasionally local officials as well, typically make up a TIF committee that approves or rejects projects requesting TIF assistance.

Once the TID is created, a developer can come forward with a proposal for their project. The developer will need the correct entitlements in place before asking for TIF, but not all TIDs place the same requirements on pre-development work before a TIF proposal is made. The plan should also include building renderings, budgets, and the project's current capital structure and shortfall.

As mentioned above, most states' TIF statutes include a "but for" test, according to which development can occur at the proposed level only when TIF funds are made available. A project would be ineligible for TIF if it is feasible without it; otherwise, the developer can move forward without needing the city's financial assistance. It is worth keeping in mind that many of these developments occur in blighted areas, where soil contamination and other factors can complicate construction or up-and-coming neighborhoods where demand is speculative, and also that many TIF projects include an affordable housing component. There complicating factors that surround these deals, thus placing them in the position where the market cannot adequately support their weight. Also, keep in mind that taxes and regulations (such as soil requirements, building ordinances, and setbacks) create market distortions. For instance, both Washington, DC, and Madison, Wisconsin, have building height restrictions, which can prevent developers from being able to build to the needs of the downtown area, as they are only allowed to construct so many stories.

The City then reviews the developer's submitted proposal. Typically, there is a person or committee that analyzes deals and rejects undesirable proposals before the projects are reviewed and approved by the TIF committee. Ideally, this person or committee is intimately familiar with the ins and outs of the real estate industry. For this book, the initial reviewer(s) (not the final TIF committee) will be referred to as the "analyst".

The first step for the city is valuing the project. The value might decrease initially if an existing, functioning structure needs to be demolished before construction of the project can begin, but should increase significantly upon completion of the improvements. The correct valuation of the proposed development is critical because the new tax basis upon completion is the foundation for the TID to calculate available TIF monies. Typically the city will employ a consultant, either full-time or ad hoc, to independently appraise the project. The developer and the city may not come to the same conclusion about the project's completed value, but the TIF committee is not required to take the developer's valuation into account when valuing the project, or at any point during the process of determining whether or not to support the development with TIF monies.

Once the analyst has established the value of the project, the difference in current tax revenue and the increased tax revenue from the project must be determined. This, called the *tax increment*, is the most critical part of a TIF project analysis because it determines the amount of TIF funds available for the city to distribute to the developer. For instance, the city may currently receive property taxes based on the existing property value of $500,000, and the new development will increase the property value to $4,200,000, a difference of $3,700,000. As you can see in Fig. 4.2 which shows a hypothetical example of a TID, this translates to tens of thousands of dollars in additional in tax revenue.

If the city approves the project, after an intensive review process, which we will go over shortly, then the city can offer a financing package for that amount to the developer, and take the increment as payment back on that financing. Municipalities then get a loan or issue bonds and hand those funds over to the developer. Municipalities that are financially strong are often able to borrow at lower interest rates than developers may be able to do. The developer then makes a payment back on these funds by just paying their taxes.

To make things more concrete, we continue the example from Fig. 4–2. In this case, the original tax basis before the TID is created is $500,000. After the project is completed, the tax basis is expected to increase by $3,700,000 to $4,200,000. Suppose, real property is taxed at the millage rate of 0.02. Then, the growth in annual property tax revenue, or the tax increment, will be $74,000. Suppose further that the TID is created for 20 years, and the city can borrow at 5.95% interest. Then, doing simple mortgage math, we find that the maximum the city can borrow (or issue bonds for) is $852,230. The city then borrows the $852,230 and hands the money over to the developer. For the next 20 years, the developer makes property tax payments of $84,000 to the city, which uses $74,000 of that to service the debt. The remaining $10,000 (the original property tax) continues to be divided among the various taxing entities (in this example: local, county, school district, vocational, technical and adult education district). Table 4.1 below summarizes the numbers discussed in our model.

The process we just described in the paragraph above (the city borrows money or issues bonds, and services the debt with tax increment payments) is the traditional and still the more popular method of tax increment financing. Recently a second method known as developer-financed TIF (or sometimes "pay as you go"), has emerged, which shifts some of the liability from municipalities to the developers. Under this method, the city does *not* borrow money or issue bonds but rather refunds almost all (about 95%) of the tax increment to the developer, who gets a loan in the

Creation of Tax Increment Districts

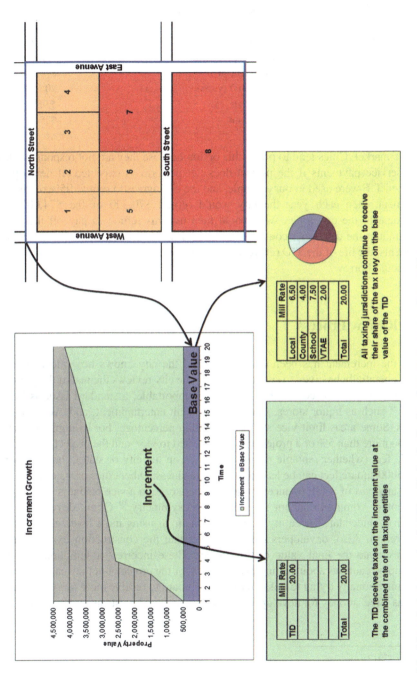

Fig. 4.2 A hypothetical example of a TID, with the distribution of tax revenues to various entities

Table 4.1 Assumptions of the TIF model

Original tax basis	$500,000
Original property tax at mill rate of 20%	$10,000
New tax basis	$4,200,000
New property tax at mill rate of 20%	$84,000
Tax basis increment	$3,700,000
Tax increment	$74,000
Life of TID (years)	20
Interest rate	5.95%
TIF amount	$852,230.14

private market. Cities tend to prefer this option because they are not responsible for debt service payments if the project does not perform as expected. If developer-financed TIF were used in our example, and the city agrees to refund 95% of the tax increment, then each year the city would refund $70,300 of the $74,000 tax increment to the developer, who would then use this refund to pay off the loan. The amount the developer could borrow would depend on the annual debt service payments, the life of the TID (20 years in our example), and the interest rate at which they could borrow.

The Review Process

Once the increment has been determined, and the city knows how much money could potentially be given to support the deal, the city reviews the rest of the project. The project must, of course, be viable and supportable; a standard issue is "vice stores"[9] such as liquor stores, smoke shops, adult entertainment, and even tanning salons. Some areas limit vice stores to a certain percentage. For example, if a city says no more than 5% of a project can be allocated to vice, and the project is 100,000 square feet (whether rentable or gross depends on the city or state), then no more than 5000 square feet can be leased to a vice business. Other cities or states refuse to allow any part of a TIF financed project to rent space to a vice business.

Another common concern is information asymmetry.[10] Often, developers are known to understate the equity available to them, as using more leverage increases their return. Also, developers can often overstate the construction expenses and underestimate the final value of the project. These incorrect assumptions can be made to be cautious about setting expectations for the project, but they can also stem from intentionally trying to mislead to the TIF board to receive more funds, as TIF is seen as "free" money for developers.[11] The review board must carefully consider the

---

[9]Weber (2013).
[10]See Luque (2018).
[11]Briffault (2010).

project's current capital structure. Any budget shortfalls should be covered by finding additional debt or (more often) equity before TIF is utilized. Only when a budget shortfall cannot be addressed by private (non-government) sources of capital should TIF be considered. This is why the TIF reviewer must carefully analyze the project's estimated value upon completion or stabilization, all construction expenses, and all sources of capital. A less common scenario occurs when a developer underestimates the construction expenses or complications of a project. This causes significant issues when TIF is involved, as there is nothing worse than a city distributing TIF to a developer only to have the entire project stalled. Thus, it is of the utmost importance that TIF reviewers have a thorough knowledge of the real estate industry.

Citizens have their concerns about the financial prudence of TIF: TIF monies are funds that would usually be used to benefit the taxpayers, by funding schools, roads, fire stations, and other municipal necessities. If the local government is going to forgo funds that could improve those vital services, then the development receiving TIF needs to be making significant improvements to the district. Will the project increase local property values by improving linkages? Will it bring jobs? Will it improve quality of life for area citizens? Or will a TIF project destroy the integrity of a neighborhood? Will it bring in new dwellers or retail that the local infrastructure cannot support? These are valid questions often asked by the taxpayers of a city, who have every right to be concerned. The TIF review board needs to take the concerns of its citizens seriously and address them throughout the review process. If TIF funds are not being used wisely or efficiently, then citizens are vindicated in their concerns.

An appearance of favoritism can also cause headaches for both the citizens and the city government. Because the TIF system can be so complicated, developers who have experience with TIF will bring forward more thorough proposals, and be more intimately aware of the city's objectives for TIDs. Experience can lead to expertise. As a result, often developers who have been awarded TIF in the past will receive it again. Some in the real estate industry say that the TIF system gives an unfair advantage to the developers who know the process well, and monies are awarded to developers based on the thoroughness of their proposals and saying the right thing, and not necessarily the merit of their project. Whether or not this sort of favoritism exists has long been a subject of debate, but the fact remains that TIF reviewers are under a high level of public scrutiny from not only citizens and other government officials, but from the real estate industry as well.

Given all of the potential for TIF to be misused or misapplied, causing waste at the very least and creating additional problems for struggling neighborhoods at the worst, there have been many calls for the end of TIF, and for communities to allow the market to determine development on its own. However, TIF does ease some of the frictions within the market to bring about needed supply; conflicts that are often created from zoning, regulation, or misuse of land or funds.

TIF from the Developer's Perspective

Most cities and tenants expect affordable housing to be built just like market-rate housing, without trimming on construction costs, since such a practice cuts the potential vacancy rate of the development dramatically. An excellent example of this particular strategy would be the Overlook Hilldale multifamily project in Madison, WI, which is one hundred percent affordable housing and even boasts renewable energy resources on the roof of the development. For this project HUD designated funds to the OHA, there was a construction loan in the WHEDA structure that was levied for the project, and other financial arrangements allowed the developer to contribute very little equity.

In an ideal model, a developer can combine their funding structures to essentially contribute no equity and cutting the potential debt service coverage ratio of their budget as well. Hence, tax increment financing is a developer's dream come true. In developments where the value of the property will likely spike to degrees far beyond where the developer could afford to pay the tax, it is reasonable to ask for some subsidy from the local government. The subsidy should theoretically be granted in exchange for developing the land, especially if that development is an affordable housing structure, and especially if that structure is an accessible housing structure for elderly residents, from the perspective of many small developers. In the United States, the number of retirees and senior citizens continues to grow. Furthermore, the majority of Americans are not saving enough for a comfortable retirement. The combination of these two factors suggests that the need for affordable retirement housing will keep growing shortly.

As we noted earlier in this chapter, the City of Madison marks out TID districts that are eligible for new development in each development cycle. These are the sites that the city considers to be ideal, and are marked eligible for TIF. Some of the TID districts can be large, and others can be quite small. Monroe Commons, for example, a building that contains residential housing and a Trader Joe's outlet grocery store is a very small TID that is just the single block plot of land that the building belongs to.

It is important to remember that different municipalities will structure their TID districts differently. For example, the small nearby village of DeForest has a very different definition of the concept of the long-term growth of the community than the City of Madison does. All towns have expansion plans and agreements about which territories can be annexed for expansion of the municipality. However, it is highly unlikely that the comparatively low-cost land of newly added plots will qualify for TID districts in coming years, so they are not wise plots to establish site control over in this case. More ideal are plots that are in middle income or lower-middle-income residential neighborhoods, where the possibility for mixed-income development is much more probable, and the location is much closer to services.[12]

It is vital to note that if you develop a property and the property tax of a neighborhood increases dramatically, the benefits for the wider community are

---

[12] See Dokow and Luque (2018).

Table 4.2 Assumptions of the simple TIF example

Current property tax	$47,000
New property tax	$270,000
Tax increment	$223,000
Life of TID (years)	23
Interest rate	5.20%
TIF amount	$2,952,052

tremendous. Property tax is the primary source of income for many areas for the basic services that they provide, including, but not at all limited to, their public education systems. Hence, municipalities, states, and federal agencies have wanted to create incentives for developers to increase the property tax of their local areas for decades.

The municipal government dictates the number of years that they will agree to use TIF. The City of Madison's sweet spot is about 15 years. But, the outcome of this is that you stabilize the property tax base of a neighborhood for a specific area. The advantage is that the property tax cannot decline at all. However, the disadvantage, often from the perspective of a few vocal individuals at the local Neighborhood Association, is that it won't allow the property tax value to increase at all.

In other words, if the assessed property tax would allow you to capitalize on a specific property tax rate the local municipality may get half of that assessed amount for the duration of the TID, so there should be some other form of service that the affordable housing development is offering to the neighborhood in exchange. But, the payoffs can be substantial. An additional simple example is shown in Table 4.2 below.

In this example, the building (or buildings) in the area designated as a TID currently pay $47,000 in property taxes annually. When the proposed development within the TID is completed, the annual property tax is expected to be $270,000. Thus, the tax increment is $223,000—the property tax would be higher by $223,000 per year due to the new development. The TID will close after 23 years. Assuming the city can borrow at 5.20% interest, the total TIF amount would be about $2.95 million, as shown in the table. The city would give this amount to the developer at the start of the project. This is a big boon for the developer, because they would have to pay the same property tax regardless of whether the project is within a TID. The difference is that the developer gets a large injection of cash ($2.95 million in our example) if the project is within the boundaries of a TID. Therefore from the perspective of developers, TIF is often a necessity for financially feasibility, as TIF funds reduce the required loan amount, and thus the annual debt service.

TIF from the Perspective of Policy Makers

TIF programs have different understandings from the perspective of policymakers, depending on whether these policymakers work with urban planning, in local governance, in municipal management, as well as if they have executive roles or legislative roles. Officials in executive functions tend to put forward their stances a bit more, although they are charged with representing the best interests of the local city or county. Officials in legislative roles will have to debate the implications of policy and work with urban planning committees. Furthermore, legislative officials will tend to have a more rounded view of the TIF programs. Some committee members might have essential criticisms of the TIF programs, while others might speak very much to positive aspects of the program. Both officials and developers would benefit most from understanding more about the nuances of how each of these positions interprets TIF.

From the perspective of municipal level governance, TIF is a critical financing tool for affordable housing development. The challenge posed by tax rates for local governments is that if they lower their tax rate on commercial centers, they will also be cutting their ability to put funds toward TIF programs. Hence, the increased tax funds from more businesses that come with lower tax rates would, in no way, make up for the lost funds by lowering the tax rate. This means that city level governance structures have often put a lot of energy into refining how TIF works, and, they make excellent resources for developers who are beginning to work on the research aspect of an affordable housing development plan. The viewpoint of municipal urban planning committee workers will confirm this position, although they are also likely to advocate that a robust capital stack will increase the likelihood that a project is financed. For example, an urban planning committee will look most favorably on a TIF application that includes other sources of funding, such as city grants, LIHTC (discussed in Chap. 3), and a realistic portrayal of the number and amount of loans needed to finance a project.

Some urban areas, such as Madison, have been particularly successful with TIF programs, and they will be more likely to have a well-oiled process for TIF applications. Hence, locating an ideal city for development is critical in this process. There are new ideas about the development of small-cap TIF programs for mixed-income affordable housing developments that have begun to circulate, so developers should keep an eye out for these programs. As we move out into the consideration of smaller urban areas as well as sub-urban perspectives on TIF, we encounter more critical takes on the program. Smaller government structures do not have as large as a tax base. Furthermore, they are much more likely, in the case of county-level governance, to see tracts of land marked for rapid private development, such as through new construction single family homes, dramatically increasing the property tax value of that tract of land.

While in the case of city level governance, the need for affordable housing is so drastic that the city is likely to waive the consideration of property tax base short-term contributions in favor of long-term development, smaller communities may be more reluctant to do so. They rely much more directly on the property tax base for funds for the public K-12 school system, the local technical college, and the county budget as a whole. Since property tax is a much higher contributor to the funds of the county budget, it would be useful for developers to keep this in mind when working with the county level authorities. Furthermore, when more funds are available to the developer to put into the initial development plan, this might allow the developer to explore innovative construction options, which would be highly favored by local communities. For example, developers could consider thinking about working the use of enamel cellulose, which could be a replacement for plastic—could be wood—could be used for cloth, glass, everything in an automobile except the engine and the tires, into their development projects. Enamel cellulose is being developed by the forest products lab in Wisconsin, is a means to think about alternative construction for the sake of long-term communal health. Another method is to think about the usage of trees on the property: two trees support life for four people if contained. They save on cooling costs, CO reduction, sequester CO_2, increase curb appeal value, and increase runoff reduction. These are just two examples. But, now, there are much more housing developments that can be tapped to in new constructions, even in the affordable housing market, than there were in previous years and decades in the industry.

Conclusion

In closing, we might constructively think of a scenario where a developer might go into a neighborhood and propose a TIF development. The question becomes: How to deal with the selling of the TIF at a neighborhood association when they look at the equations, and they read it as decreased value for the school district because you essentially fix the property tax for 15 years, when they think it might increase. The argument for the long-term health of the greater community must be presented. TIF, in this case, is one way to point toward long-term community health concerning the market that extends beyond the individual neighborhood association.

Although the TIF tax credits are allocated by the state, the state takes 1/13th and multiplies by a million to establish the federal share. A tax credit is a dollar for dollar addition to the bottom line of the development plan. The deductions are a function of the tax rate. But the savings and the financials of the development can be put into other new investments. Furthermore, having a bit of flexibility and with these funds means that a developer might be able to pursue more innovative construction techniques. While we turn to the structures of city grants in the following chapter, readers will notice that we do not discount these considerations of the environment of development, primarily since they will remain important in following chapters.

References

Briffault R (2010) The most popular tool: tax increment financing and the political economy of local government. The University of Chicago Law Review 77:65–95

Cassell MK, Turner RC (2010) Racing to the bottom? the impact of intrastate competition on tax abatement generosity in Ohio. State and Local Government Review 42(3):195–209

Council of Development Finance Agencies (2015) Tax increment finance state-by-state report

Dokow E, Luque J (2018) Provision of local public goods in mixed income communities. J Hous Econ. https://doi.org/10.1016/j.jhe.2018.02.005

Dye RF, Merriman DF (2006) Tax increment financing: a tool for local economic development. Journal of Housing and Community Development 63(3):22

Ingraham AT, Singer HJ, Thibodeau TG (2005) Inter-city competition for retail trade: can tax increment financing generate incremental tax receipts? Available SSRN https://ssrn.com/abstract=766925 or https://doi.org/10.2139/ssrn.766925. Accessed 22 July 2005

Lefcoe G, Swenson CW (2014) Redevelopment in California: The demise of TIF-funded redevelopment in California and its aftermath. Natl Tax J 67:719–744

Luque J (2018) Assessing the role of TIF and LIHTC in an equilibrium model of affordable housing development. Reg Sci Urban Econ. https://doi.org/10.1016/j.regsciurbeco.2018.06.005

Weber R (2013) Tax increment financing in theory and practice. Financing Economic Development in the 21st Century, 53, 55

Chapter 5
Housing the Homeless

Abstract In this chapter, we explain the business model and difficulties of non-profit organizations specialized in providing homeless shelters and housing for homeless and vulnerable populations. We focus on the case of Porchlight, an organization based in Madison, Wisconsin, to highlight the importance of case management, location and development size. We also discuss the main challenges to house different types of homeless people, such as chronic homeless, veteran homeless, and homeless children. Along these discussions, we offer some facts and figures regarding market rents, the barriers to permanent housing for the homeless, and interstate homeless migration flows for the case of Madison, Wisconsin (Facts and figures are used with permission from Karla Thennes, Executive Director of Porchlight). Throughout this chapter we aim to develop a better sense of the needs of the populations who would ideally live in affordable housing developments, so that developers can be better prepared to create successful plans.

Porchlight: An Introduction

Porchlight focuses on providing homeless shelters and housing for homeless and housing vulnerable populations. They also work substantially with case managers and service providers for their residents, since they have found that to prevent a re-emergence into homelessness, recently housed populations frequently need substantial support. The community in Madison, Wisconsin, has rallied strongly around the issue of providing support for homeless families, meaning that the community feels like it does better on the issue of homelessness than comparable cities. That said, Porchlight provides housing to the niche service population of chronically homeless single men, a still substantially underserved people in the City of Madison. This has been their significant contribution to the Madison community over their decades of work.

While Porchlight mostly focuses on running a shelter for homeless single men and providing permanent affordable housing for the formerly homeless, it also runs several other programs serving the homeless and vulnerable populations. Figure 5.1 describes Porchlight's major programs.

Program	Description
Drop-in shelter	Men's drop-in shelter, at Grace Episcopal Church
DIGS	Eviction prevention program
Safe Haven	Housing and day services for adults with mental illnesses
Affordable housing	25 properties with almost 350 housing units (SROs, efficiencies, one bedrooms, family units)
Porchlight Products	Employment and job training program

Fig. 5.1 List and description of Porchlight programs. Source: Porchlight

Porchlight has almost 350 units of affordable housing, which they also levy to support the housing-vulnerable populations in Madison. Porchlight is recognized by the local community as one of the leaders in providing substantial services, property management, and case management to their residents. This leadership has emerged from a series of strategic decisions at the governance level. Having centralized control over the issue of case management and property management with their particular tenants' needs, has given Porchlight more appropriate control over situations than if there was outside property management. Also important for their success have been the careful choice of locations for their housing. Figure 5.2 shows the locations of Porchlight's properties.

Porchlight's Considerations Regarding Housing Location and Size

Porchlight's criteria for selecting locations are the following. First, housing must be close to reliable public transportation, within only a couple of blocks walk to a bus stop. Second, developments for single men's housing tend to be around commercial buildings, meaning that the housing is pushed to high-risk neighborhoods for populations that are particularly vulnerable to health and safety concerns.

There are many considerations to keep in mind by a developer of affordable housing. Here we highlight some of these considerations. First, a developer seeking to build housing for single men in a residential neighborhood would receive substantial pushback. One possibility to make it work is to target a low-income population that is not the poorest of the poor. Another possibility for the developer is to target pre-existing low-income housing developments that are either expanded or adapted.

Regarding the optimal size of housing developments for the homeless, research shows that they tend to be quite small to allow for adequate funds to be devoted to the substantial services that they need to provide. For a mid-size city such as Madison, an ideal maximum would be a 16-unit building of efficiencies, and no more than 5–8 units in a mixed-income development of 50 units. Although in some models a 60-unit building is possible, such a large structure devoted entirely to

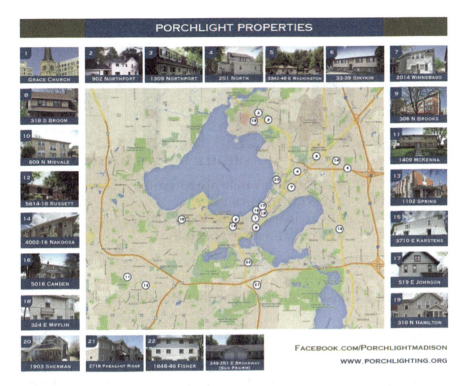

Fig. 5.2 Locations of Porchlight's properties in Madison and Dane County. Source: Porchlight

housing the homeless is a significant burden for the needs and balance of the community. In the case of a mixed-income development, 4–5 units would be much easier to manage, and families are easier to handle than single men. But in these cases, location is even more critical as half of the families will not have transportation themselves, and 8 units of three bedrooms each would be the most that a case manager would recommend in a single location.

An important consideration regarding the choice of location of a community center is that it has to be nearby the development to cover the Out of School Time (OST) of the children, particularly in cases where there are not extended family around to care for children. Porchlight has therefore built substantial playground equipment in some of their units, as the communal space makes it possible for the families to be more a part of the collective unit structure. If there is daycare onsite, it is ideal for families. If the location is nearby Madison School Community Recreational (MSCR) centers, it is also ideal, although it is essential to keep in mind that the families that are being served may need additional services. All this said, it is crucial to keep in mind that Madison is a comparatively well-served community, by national standards, and even by regional standards.

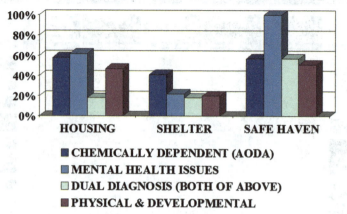

Fig. 5.3 Shares of Porchlight residents and guests with various disabilities. Source: Porchlight

Porchlight's Considerations Regarding Housing Services

The most important part of maintaining Porchlight services, particularly for homeless single men, is a realistic appraisal of the necessary costs and challenges of the program. For example, at one of Porchlight's developments, which received $200,000 from the city for the building and a HUD grant of $150,000 for case management services, and is made up of 10 efficiencies for chronically homeless men, almost all the individuals in the development have struggled with drug addiction in recent years. As Fig. 5.3 shows, drug and alcohol dependency is common among Porchlight guests. The data in the chart are based on self-reported answers, so these numbers likely understate the pervasiveness of chemical dependency and mental health issues among the homeless.

The location only has one full-time case manager, one part-time case manager, and one part-time drug counselor, for staff. One common problem non-profits like Porchlight face is that it can be difficult to retain talented employees such as case managers and counselors. This is predominantly because Porchlight cannot typically offer the highest wages, and employees often leave for higher wages elsewhere. Also, some employees leave due to the stress of working in an environment with high drug use.

Of all of Porchlight's units, 50–60 units require Porchlight to take from the city list of individuals in immediate need of housing. The program follows the "VI-SPDAT"—assessing the vulnerability of the homeless population, a survey developed by OrgCode Consulting, Inc. VI-SPDAT consists of several dozen personal questions, meaning that the nature of the question, by reputation, could turn some individuals away. Furthermore, Porchlight cannot select those individuals from the list who would make ideal candidates. As an organization, they are bound by regulations to only intake the top individuals on the list. Consequentially, they consistently take the most difficult cases.

This means that Porchlight inevitably ends up with some "problem tenants". Many of the tenants' active drug use that is a barrier to the stability of healthcare and employment. Many have records of recent criminal activity. Despite their best intentions, occasionally Porchlight is forced to evict a problem tenant or two because their encounters with the police disrupt the lives of other tenants. However, the city's rules can make it difficult to evict tenants. To make matters even more difficult, Porchlight is currently facing a question about the stability of their *HUD* funding and faces further difficulties. They continuously face questions that are seemingly very basic, but reveal structural problems associated with managing individual cases in the circumstances of Madison's homeless population: *What is a reasonable population for a building? What type of problems are associated with homeless housing? What type of developments work for homeless and what kind don't work?*

Emergency Shelters

Porchlight runs the only temporary emergency shelter for single men in Madison. Other organizations (such as The Salvation Army) run shelters for single women and families. The single men's shelter is located in the basement of Grace Episcopal Church in downtown Madison and was started when two men froze to death on a cold winter night in the 1980s. Due to limited space and resources, the men's shelter will only house a single individual for 90 nights in the year, although an extreme weather exemption is given when temperatures drop below 20 degrees. Guests receive two hot meals per day, which is supplied and served by over 60 volunteer organizations and more than 1000 individual volunteers throughout the year. During winter months, the emergency shelter serves about 160–180 men per night. Figure 5.4 shows the total number of men who stayed at the shelter in 1986–2016.

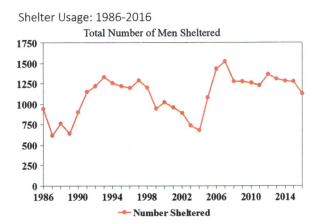

Fig. 5.4 Number of men sheltered at Porchlight shelter, 1986–2016. Source: Porchlight

Homeless Veterans

The City of Madison has recently joined the nation-wide initiative to eliminate homelessness among veterans by the end of 2017. A number of local non-profit organizations, including Porchlight, have joined the coordinated effort to make sure no veteran is homeless in Dane County. Although there are still more than 30 individuals in the city of Madison who are homeless veterans, the community has made significant progress in this area, considering that there were almost 170 homeless veterans when the initiative was launched.

Chronic Homelessness

Thinking about the potential causes of these situations, for these families, or for any of the individuals, we have to ask the question: *what is the cause of chronic homelessness?* In most situations, there tend to be mental health and substance abuse issues. In addition to these two issues, single veterans are also more likely to have post-traumatic stress disorder (PTSD). Depression, anxiety, and stress are also common for such populations. These are strongly related to homelessness, and, often, there is a sense that secure housing might treat at least the first layer of these issues. Figure 5.5 shows the self-reported statistics on the various health issues of Madison's unsheltered population in 2012–2016.

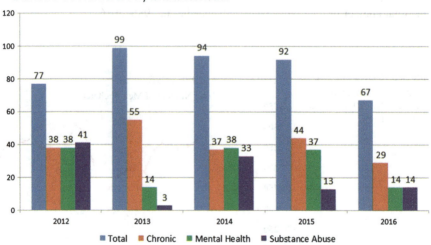

Fig. 5.5 The unsheltered homeless population in Madison by characteristics. Categories are self-reported. Source: Porchlight, January Point-In Time Surveys (2012–2016)

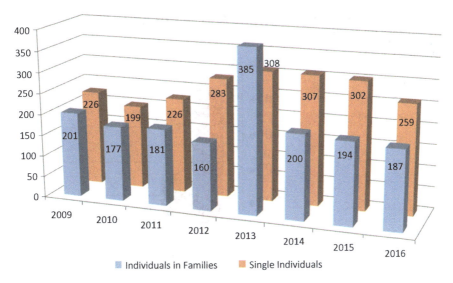

Fig. 5.6 Analysis of the homeless population by household type. Family data includes 0–7 unaccompanied youth. Source: Porchlight, January Point-In Time Surveys (2009–2015)

Breakdown of Homeless Individuals By Household Type in Madison

While the common perception of a homeless person is a single man, there are significant numbers of single women and individuals in families. Data from the Point-In-Time surveys from 2009 to 2015 show the breakdown of homeless individuals by household type in Madison (See Fig. 5.6).

Free Mobility: Does Madison, WI, Attract Homeless From Other States?

One of the dilemmas that city and state governments argue they face is that improving services for the homeless can attract more homeless or housing vulnerable people from rural areas, other cities, or states. Even if a city starts out by attempting to solve its homelessness problem, offering more support and services may eventually require continued expansion of such services. This is potentially a problem that Madison, WI faces. Because Madison has more services and support for the homeless relative to other cities in the region, critics have suggested it attracts lots of homeless individuals from nearby cities like Chicago. However, our available data do not seem to support this claim. Based on the most recent data available, which is from 2012, it is undoubtedly the case that the majority of the homeless population are not arriving in Madison from Chicago. As Figs. 5.7, 5.8 and 5.9 show,

Fig. 5.7 Previous addresses of Porchlight family shelter guests, 2012. Source: Porchlight, Servicepoint data based on 1219 responses

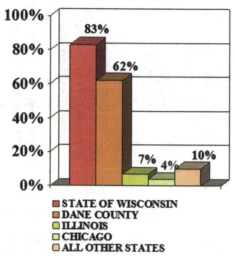

Fig. 5.8 Previous addresses of Porchlight family shelter guests, 2012. Source: Porchlight, Servicepoint data based on 323 responses

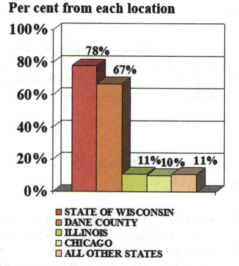

the majorities of homeless single men, single women, and families in Madison are in fact from Dane County and the State of Wisconsin. Among men 83% are from Wisconsin, and only 7% are from Chicago. Among women, 78% are from Wisconsin, and 67% are from Dane County. The number of transplants from Illinois is higher for families, at 18%.

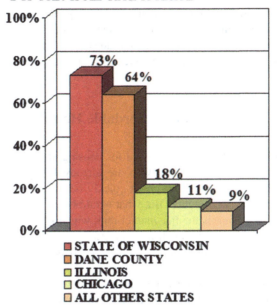

Fig. 5.9 Previous addresses of Porchlight family shelter guests, 2012. Source: Porchlight, Servicepoint data based on 1037 responses

Homeless as a Working Class: Barriers to Access Permanent Housing

By contrast with some other rental agencies, Porchlight only requires an individual to make twice the monthly rent per month, but this is still a substantial cost. Furthermore, if we are to think about the theoretical problem of moving those in Porchlight shelters into more permanent homes, we would have to ask: *how many of those in Porchlight housing are working full-time?*

At the men's shelter in Madison, Wisconsin, roughly 30% of the guests work some part-time position, which is a higher number than some might expect. Nonetheless, this population often faces the difficulty of having an additional background history of poor credit, or a criminal history from several years ago (sometimes 15 or more years ago), which makes it difficult to rent an apartment. Another difficulty is the references of landlords. In the past, landlords in the City of Madison could only check a tenant's criminal history for the previous 2 years. Currently, landlords can check for a lifetime of criminal records. Job training is a desperate need for this population, although it is important to note that a small, but significant, number of the members of this community receive disability checks of about $750/month. Hence, if these checks could be coupled with a substantial part-time position, the ability to afford an apartment would be much more feasible. However, it is not necessarily realistic to expect this of potential tenants. Disability income is decided on a case by case basis, and considering these factors only further underscores the need for developers to take the need for access to caseworkers and other individual concerns into consideration during all stages of the planning process. One of the difficulties that the population and the organization case managers face is that there is a very limited supply of permanent affordable housing in the City of Madison and Dane County. For example, in Madison, Wisconsin, the wait list for public housing or Sect. 8 housing choice vouchers is at least 3 years.

Market Rents and Affordable Housing in Madison

All of this highlights the need for housing at affordable rents, in part to house the population of homeless who are already living in the area, and those housing vulnerable people who could quickly become homeless with a missed rent check and an eviction notice. But what would be affordable housing in Madison? A good starting point is the fair market rent, which is the estimate of gross rent in a given metropolitan or nonmetropolitan areas.[1]

Currently, fair market rent is calculated as the 40th percentile rent, and can thus be considered slightly below-average rent in a given market (U.S. Department of Housing and Urban Development 2007). In 2017, fair market rents for Dane County were $673/month for an efficiency, $813/month for a one-bedroom, $964/month for a two-bedroom, $1342/month for a three-bedroom, and $1549/month for a four-bedroom unit. Alarmingly, fair market rents for Dane County have increased by at least 13% in just 1 year. For example, fair market rent is $924/month for a one-bedroom unit and $1091/month for a two-bedroom unit in 2018.

Tenants often need savings equal to at least several times the monthly rent to be able to get an apartment. Furthermore, affordability means not spending most of their monthly income on rent. For example, landlords often require the tenants to make three times the assessed rent of an apartment per month. For an individual who makes $10/hour, even a studio apartment would have to be only $480/month to be affordable. A person who makes $20/hour full time would need to find a place that is under $960/month. In other words: a person working full-time at $20/hour would only barely be able to afford a one-bedroom apartment in Madison. It is important to consider that all of these assessments are made based on pre-tax income, and if they were made based on post-tax income, housing costs eat up even larger shares of tenants' incomes. Figure 5.10 shows fair market rents in Dane County (left panel) and the monthly wages and maximum affordable rents (right panel).

---

[1]FMRs are estimated by the U.S. Department of Housing and Urban Development, and "are primarily used to determine payment standard amounts for the Housing Choice Voucher program, to determine initial renewal rents for some expiring project-based Sect. 8 contracts, to determine initial rents for housing assistance payment (HAP) contracts in the Moderate Rehabilitation Single Room Occupancy program (Mod Rehab), and to serve as a rent ceiling in the HOME rental assistance program." See the HUD document "Fair Market Rents: Overview".

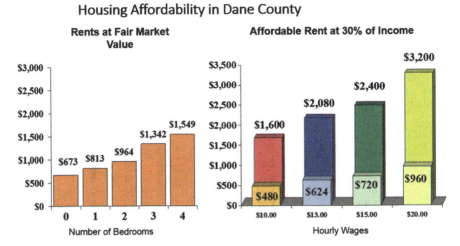

Fig. 5.10 Fair market and affordable rent levels in Dane County. The left panel shows the fair market rents for efficiency to four-bedroom units for 2017. The right panel shows the monthly pre-tax wages at various hourly wage rates, as well as the maximum gross rent affordable using the 30% rule of thumb. Source: HUD & National Low Income Coalition

To compare Madison rents to surrounding areas, consider fair market rates for 2017. As Fig. 5.11 shows, monthly rent for an efficiency was $673/month in Madison, compared to $615 in Milwaukee and $539 in Racine. Fair market rent for a four-bedroom apartment was $1549/month in Madison, significantly higher than the $1311 in Milwaukee, and $1070 in Racine. Furthermore, as mentioned above, fair market rents rose at least 13% in Dane County from 2017 to 2018, making housing even less affordable for low-income households and individuals.

Of course, rent is one half of the housing affordability story; the other is income. In 2017, in Dane County, the median income for a family of four was $82,600, and $57,900 for a single person. Whether the individuals who live in Porchlight housing work full-time or part-time, or rely on disability checks, the overwhelming majority has very low income, relative to the county average. As Fig. 5.12 shows, 92% of Porchlight residents have incomes that are at or below 30% of county median income. About 8% (mostly veterans) have incomes that are between 30% and 50% of county median income, and none have an above-average income.

It is unlikely that these individuals will somehow ever manage to bootstrap their way into a stable housing situation by their means alone. Hence, initiatives to help the homeless population are critical. Porchlight works extensively with veterans, and it is important to note that, as long as there is a case manager to help the individual fill out the necessary paperwork, full veterans' benefits are substantial compared to non-veterans' benefits.

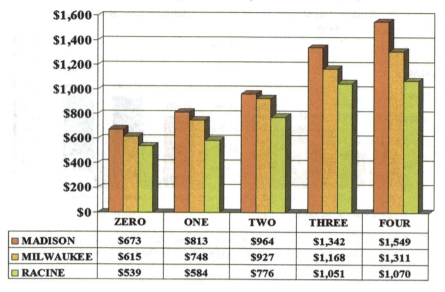

Fig. 5.11 Comparison of fair market rents for Madison, Milwaukee, and Racine in 2017. Source: HUD

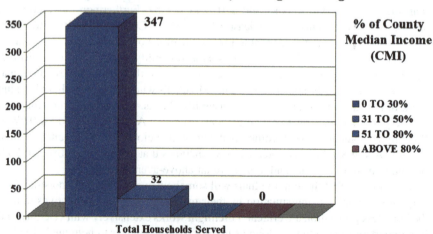

Fig. 5.12 Income levels of Porchlight residents as compared to the county median income. Source: Porchlight

The Way to Pay for Services for the Homeless Is to Run Affordable Housing Programs

Case management and the consideration of the Porchlight model go hand in hand. Because of the nature of the cases that they deal with, and because of the policies that they must comply with, along with other restrictions and features of their service niche, Porchlight builds a 10% vacancy and collection losses into their model, meaning that they assume that they cannot account for 10% of the income of their rental units. This is mostly because their turnover rate is substantial.

This model of housing requires a substantial staff. As a result, Porchlight employs a housing team, a property management team, and an eviction prevention team. It requires housing staff of three full-time staff and three part-time staff, with roughly one full-time case manager for 30 people, or for 15 families. Even still, the largest source of revenue for the organization is rent paid by tenants. Much of their overhead costs are covered by state and federal agencies, certainly. But, the rent that people pay into the organization is critical for the funding of their various programs. However, they must invest substantially in case management to prevent evictions. The costs of evictions are substantial for landlords, and the humanitarian cost, for their model, is unquestionably high if they are forced to evict one of their tenants. They, therefore, attempt to avoid evictions at all costs. However, they also have a policy that states that they will not take co-signers, which means that they will not have relatives of homeless populations taking care of them. This has costs and benefits. One of the costs is that the organization is faced with writing off debt on a regular basis. For example, Porchlight currently writes off more than $100,000 per year in bad debt per year. However, we should also note that they do not necessarily mind this number. This is essentially one of the services of their programs, debt forgiveness, for the sake of long-term individual and community health. Debt forgiveness, after all, only amounts to less than 3% percent of their roughly $5 million per year budget. Given that they have a staff of 100, they foresee that the greatest budgetary increase, in an ideal world, would be to add more staff for their units. More recently these costs have necessarily expanded as wages have increased as well. Ideally, Porchlight would like to encourage a certain amount of feasible mixed-income housing for homeless individuals, at the rate of 8 out of a total of 50 units. The question for the location of these developments would be: Where are community centers? Where are the boys' and girls' clubs?

To illustrate the importance of these questions, let us consider a mixed-income development in the Village of Cambridge. The village is 2% unemployed, but those who are income overburdened is substantially higher than the county average. There is no public transportation in the area. What would the development need? Based on the Porchlight model, we would have to consider the location to services, such as food stamp offices, eviction prevention, and food pantries. We would have to explore the potential of the development of a ride share program. A developer might consider the establishment of a car donation program, such as in the case of Stoughton, where an individual who was a retired mechanic was able to donate more than 50 old cars to families in the area who did not have them. The Village of Cambridge is not necessarily a typical family structure compared to other areas of the city, however. The typical makeup of homeless families in Madison, for example, is the single parent. Two and three-bedroom sizes are high need groups in all low to middle-income brackets. Furthermore, many have not considered that the majority of homeless in Madison are not necessarily adults.

Homeless Children

In the Madison Metropolitan School District, about 1500 school children register as homeless at the start of each school year. When these students are included in the homeless population, the average age of a homeless person in Madison is 9 years old!

The school district uses a somewhat looser definition of homelessness than merely someone who is on the street or in a shelter. The district also counts families with unstable housing situations—those who are living in doubled-up living arrangements, or living in a hotel—in a single or shared room—since those families that are the most vulnerable and most likely to become homeless within a matter of days, weeks, or months. Caseworkers are critical in these circumstances. For example, the YWCA works with outside management. One case manager to 10 families in these cases would be the ideal working model—if those caseworkers are working with doctors and therapists. Furthermore, for homeless children, simple aspects of childhood, such as playing on sports teams or being involved with school club activities, are much more difficult. Porchlight has been able to make some goods available through consolidating donations to particularly middle-school aged students, where sports equipment can cost hundreds of dollars. In these cases, the position of the caseworker is critical in assessing the needs of the child. Occasionally grants are mustered, but these are not available on a regular basis. Based on the Porchlight model, it is important to remember that, within the consideration of caseworkers, security may also be an added cost for Porchlight locations. Furthermore, the single men population requires three full-time alcohol and drug counselors, who might make $19 an hour (the same positions could pay $65/hour in the for-profit sector). Often the individual caseworkers are recent college graduates or those without bachelor's degrees, who then move on to get their master's degree. Hence the non-profit world acts as, essentially, training for the for-profit world. For families, the same problems persist, but there is an added cost of affordable childcare for second and third shift hours. Often there is a drawing upon the retired population. One possible solution that has been suggested and received some discussion is that the city is starting to build "gran housing," and it could be the grandparents who are raising the children.

Another issue with children is that kids get "emergency sick," and so who is going to take care of the kid when you are at a factory or McDonalds? Hence, fourplex and eight-plex so that the families get together in a community in the hope that they will form a community to get together around that. Within those communities, we cannot forget, though, that the make or break individual in a family's life is often their caseworker.

Conclusion

This chapter has two main goals. The first is to highlight the additional challenges involved with providing housing and related services to the homeless population. From the perspective of developers, building market rate housing is typically the most straightforward proposition. Affordable housing is more challenging, due to the additional sources of capital that are usually needed. Within this sector, building housing for the homeless is even more challenging, due to the need for supportive services, such as case management, drug counseling, and employment services. Therefore, it is important for potential developers to have experience in this area, or at least team up with organizations that specialize in providing services for the homeless populations. The second goal of the chapter is to explain in some detail the array of services that the homeless populations require. We have done this using the example of Porchlight, Inc's activities in Madison, Wisconsin. However, the need for services and the challenges faced are fairly consistent throughout the country. More obviously, funding from both federal and local governments continues to shrink, making it difficult or impossible to reduce the number of Americans who are without stable housing.

Reference

U.S. Department of Housing and Urban Development (2007) Fair market rent: overview

Chapter 6
Financial Feasibility Analysis: Planning for the Possible

Abstract In this chapter, we discuss the concept of financial feasibility introduced by the late James Graaskamp. We also review two commonly used techniques in feasibility studies, the front-door analysis, and the back-door analysis. These concepts and techniques will be used in subsequent chapters to assess the impact of location and financial subsidies, such as Low Income Housing Tax Credits and Tax Increment Financing, on the feasibility of an affordable housing development project.

In previous chapters, we discussed in some detail the extent of the affordable housing crisis in the United States. While this is a more pressing issue in some parts of the country than in others, increasing the recent run-up in housing prices is putting a strain on a household budget (especially on renter households), in most cities. We also discussed some of the policies and practices adopted by local governments to increase the availability of housing for lower-income households. However, an affordable housing development plan will only be viable if it makes financial sense from the developer's point of view. Construction of housing involves substantial amounts of investment, including on land, labor, construction materials, as well as entrepreneurial talent. Hence, before a project is undertaken, the developer must have a reasonable expectation that the project will be feasible, in the sense that its value will be high enough to pay for land, wages, and materials, as well as to leave some profit for themselves.

Graaskamp's Financial Feasibility Model

Professor Graaskamp, who was both an academic and a practitioner, was a pioneer in the study of financial feasibility for real estate developments. He is credited with introducing a comprehensive framework and "analytical techniques to improve the reliability and accuracy of real estate feasibility analysis" (Ciochetti and Malizia

2000). According to Graaskamp (1972), a project is feasible when "there is a reasonable likelihood of satisfying explicit objectives when a selected course of action is tested for fit to a context of specific constraints and limited resources."

Thus, feasibility is a broad concept: the project must meet not only the developer's objectives but satisfy all parties involved, including lenders, regulators, and users. He further described the three everyday situations where feasibility is considered. These are:

1. A site in search of a use
2. Use in search of a site; and
3. An investor looking for a real estate opportunity

Graaskamp advocated the use of the so-called "front-door" and "back-door" analyses in feasibility studies, which are still used in the industry today (Graaskamp 1981). Although the front-door/back-door analyses are often attributed to Graaskamp, it was in fact his PhD student Jim DeLisle who first developed them. Graaskamp is responsible for popularizing the techniques through his teaching and writings. See Malpezzi (The Wisconsin program in real estate and urban land economics: a century of tradition and innovation. Washington, DC, University of Wisconsin, 2015). The front-door analysis starts with the estimate of project costs and calculates the rent required to make the project financially feasible. This model is typically used in the first type of feasibility study (a site in search of a use). The back-door analysis starts with estimated rental income a project will command and calculates the maximum supportable site acquisition cost that makes the project feasible. This model is commonly used in the second type of feasibility study (a use in search of a site).

The "site in search of a use" type of feasibility study can be used, for example, if a developer considers a specific site (which they may own) and is deciding what to build on it. For a potential development plan, she starts with project costs and calculates the required rent per unit. The front-door model is the appropriate tool to use in this scenario. The front-door model, which starts with development costs for a given site, considers the required cash flows to satisfy both debt and equity sources, and ends with required rents, can be broken down into the following steps:

As the table in Fig. 6.1 shows, the first step is to estimate the total development cost. In this case, we take the site cost as given; this is the market value of the land, whether the property must be bought, or is already in the developer's possession. The hard and soft construction costs are added to the land cost, which gives us the total development cost. In most cases, real estate development is financed with two primary sources: equity (the owner's money) and debt (other people's money). The loan-to-cost ratio determines the respective amounts of each source. This is merely the ratio of the loan amount to the total development cost. The balance of the development budget comes from the developer's own money or equity. For example, if the total development cost is $1,200,000 and the loan-to-cost ratio is 75%, then the loan would be $900,000, and the developer would contribute $300,000 of their own money. Both debt investors (lenders) and equity investors contribute funds

	Site Cost	
	+ Construction Costs (Hard and Soft)	
	= Total Development Cost	
x (1 - Loan-to-Cost Ratio)		x Loan-to-Cost Ratio
= Required Equity		= Maximum Loan Amount
x Equity Dividend Rate		x Annual Loan Constant
= Required Equity Dividend	+	= Annual Debt Service
	= Required Net Operating Income or NOI	
	+ Estimated Operating Expenses	
	= Required Effective Gross Income	
	÷ Expected Occupancy Rate	
	= Required Gross Revenue	
	÷ Leasable Square Feet or Units	
	= Rent Required Per Square Foot or Per Unit	

Fig. 6.1 The basic steps involved in the front-door analysis

with the expectation of future returns, which depend on the relative riskiness of their respective investments. Lenders have the priority claim on future cash flows, and the equity investors are paid if and when there is cash flow left over after making the debt service payments. Therefore, both risk and rate of return on debt are lower than on equity. The return that equity investors expect is called the equity dividend rate, while the return the lenders expect is the annual loan constant.[1]

The next step is to calculate the required payments to the two sources of funds. Annual debt service is the payment required to meet the debt investor's return, which is merely the loan amount multiplied by the annual mortgage constant. The required equity dividend is the amount of equity invested multiplied by the equity dividend rate. For the project to be feasible, the building must, at a minimum, generate enough cash flow to meet the required equity dividend and annual debt service payments. Required net operating income gives this amount. However, net operating income is not merely the total rent that the building is expected to generate. Some of the rent collected will go towards operating expenses, such as property taxes, property insurance, and maintenance. Furthermore, not all units of the completed building will always be occupied by tenants. Therefore, we need first to adjust the estimated operating expenses. Adding those to the net operating income will give us the required effective gross income. Next, we need to adjust the number of units that may remain vacant. This is done by dividing the effective gross income by the occupancy rate, which is just (1—vacancy rate). This adjustment gives us the required gross income, which is the maximum potential rental income the building could generate. Tenants rarely lease entire buildings but instead based on square feet of space (with retail and offices) or by unit (with apartments). Therefore, the last step in the front-door analysis is to calculate the rent required per square foot or per

---

[1] Annual loan constant is defined as the annual payment required to amortize (pay off) $1 of debt, and it depends on the term and interest rate of the loan.

	Site Cost:	$200,000
	+ Construction costs:	$1,000,000
	= Total development cost:	$1,200,000
x (1 - Loan-to-Cost Ratio): 0.25		x Loan-to-Cost Ratio: 0.75
= Required Equity: $300,000		= Maximum Loan Amount: $900,000
x Equity Dividend Rate: 0.10		x Annual Loan Constant: 0.0872
= Equity Dividend: $30,000	+	= Annual Debt Service: $78,466
	= Net Operating Income:	$108,466
	+ Operating Expenses:	$20,000
	= Effective Gross Income:	$128,466
	÷ Expected Occupancy Rate:	0.95
	= Required Gross Revenue:	$135,227
	÷ Leasable units:	8 units
	= **Rent Required Per Unit:**	**$16,903**

Fig. 6.2 Front-door analysis example for an 8-unit apartment building

unit. The question that the developer asks is: "Is this required rent per square foot or per unit achievable at this location?" If they can be confident that the answer is yes, then the project should be considered further.

To illustrate this approach with a numerical example, suppose that a developer owns a site with a market value of $200,000. He is exploring the feasibility of a small, 8-unit apartment building on the site. The hard and soft construction costs would total $1,000,000. A bank is willing to finance the project with a 0.75 loan-to-cost ratio, a 6% interest and a 20-year term, and annual payments. The remainder would come from equity investor(s), who require a 10% return. The operating expenses are expected to be $20,000 per year, and vacancy is expected to be 5%. The calculations are shown in the table in Fig. 6.2.

As the table shows, given the assumptions, this project would be feasible if each apartment could generate $16,903 in rent per year or $1409 per month. Depending on the prevailing market rents for comparable apartments, the developer may or may not decide to pursue the project.

As DeLisle and Griego (2008) points out, the front-door analysis is based on the "Field of Dreams" approach to real estate development: if you build it, they will come. While it is true that many projects are examples of such speculative development, this attitude can lead to a building that does not have sufficient demand or payment capacity. In contrast, the back-door analysis is more realistic about affordability—it starts with the rental income that the building can realistically generate. As pointed out earlier, it is not always the case that the developer owns a site or has one in mind and is looking at possible uses for that site. Sometimes, the developer already has a use in mind. For instance, the developer may:

– specialize (as most do) in certain types of projects, such as offices or apartments,
– have a tenant in mind, or
– be hired by a client to build a project.

In such cases, it is easier to start with the expected rental income, since the use is known with reasonable certainty. Thus, it is natural to use the back-door model. The

	Gross Revenue	
	− Vacancy and Collection Losses	
	= Effective Gross Income	
	− Operating Expenses	
	= Net Operating Income	
− Annual Debt Service		÷ Required Debt Coverage Ratio
= Available Equity Dividend		= Cash Available for Debt Service
÷ Required Equity Dividend Rate		÷ Annual Loan Constant
= Justified Equity Investment	+	= Justified loan amount
	= Justified Development Cost	
	− Expected Construction Costs	
	= Justified Price of Site	

Fig. 6.3 The basic steps involved in the back-door analysis

back-door model takes the prevailing market rents as a given and works backward to find the maximum site cost that would justify the project. The table in Fig. 6.3 shows the necessary steps in the process.

As the table shows, the back-door analysis starts with an estimate of the gross revenue that the expected use will generate. We then make adjustments for vacancy and collection losses, as well as operating expenses, to arrive at the net operating income (NOI). The net operating income will be split between debt service and payments to equity investors. The maximum debt service the building can support is given by the lender's lowest acceptable debt coverage ratio.[2] In turn, the maximum annual debt service, combined with the loan term and interest rate, give us the maximum loan amount that will be forthcoming. The portion of the NOI that does not go towards debt service will be equity investors' return. The combination of the expected payment to equity investors and the equity dividend rate gives us the justified equity investment. The sum of the maximum loan and equity investment give us the total development cost that can be justified by the building's rental income. After subtracting the expected construction costs, we "back into" the justified price of the site. Thus, with the back-door analysis, the developer can estimate the maximum amount for the site that would allow the project to pay the required returns for both debt and equity. If they can find a suitable location for this price or less, then the plan is potentially feasible and should be pursued.

Let's flip the same example we used for the front-door analysis to illustrate the back-door approach, and why the two may diverge. Suppose a developer who specializes in building houses (homebuilder) is considering an 8-unit apartment building and is looking for a suitable site. Average market rents are expected to be $1350 per month per unit or $129,600 annually for the entire project. As before, vacancy is 5%, and operating expenses are $20,000 per year. Lenders require a

---

[2] Debt coverage ratio is defined as: net operating income divided by annual debt service. Depending on the type of project, lenders require the debt coverage ratio to be at least 1.15–1.25, meaning the net operating income must be 15–25% more than the annual debt service.

	Potential Gross Rent:	$129,600		
	- Vacancy and Collection Losses:	$6,480		
	= Effective Gross Income:	$136,080		
	- Operating Expenses:	$20,000		
	= Net Operating Income:	$116,080		
- Annual Debt Service: $92,864			÷ Debt Coverage Ratio:	1.25
= Available Equity Dividend: $23,216			= Cash for Debt Service:	$92,864
÷ Required Equity Dividend Rate: 0.10			÷ Annual Loan Constant:	0.0872
= Justified Equity Investment: $232,160		+	= Justified loan amount:	$1,065,143
	= Development Cost:	$1,297,303		
	- Construction Costs:	$1,000,000		
	= **Justified Price of Site:**	**$297,303**		

Fig. 6.4 Back-door analysis example for an 8-unit apartment building

minimum debt coverage ratio of 1.15 and are willing to offer 20-year loans with annual payments, at 6%. Given the risks involved, the required equity dividend rate is 10%. The table in Fig. 6.4 shows the relevant calculations.

The table shows that given the market rents that the building is expected to generate, and the other assumptions, the project will only be feasible if the site can be bought for slightly less than $300,000. If the developer can secure a suitable location for less, the project is viable and should be considered further. On the other hand, if land prices are much higher in the current market, the plan is infeasible and should be abandoned.

Careful readers will note that both front-door and back-door analyses are based on annual numbers for debt and equity, which represent a return *on* the funds, rather than the return *of* the funds. This is unrealistic since a substantial portion of the overall return on most real estate investments comes from the eventual sale of the property, which will be years or decades in the future. The two approaches also ignore the time value of money. Therefore, the front-door and back-door analyses are not the only techniques that are employed in feasibility studies, or even the most comprehensive ones. They should be treated as the first step, as preliminary tests of the feasibility of a project or as screening tools to eliminate projects that are likely to fail. However, the two approaches are "fairly robust and provide a valid starting point for more advanced investment modeling including discounted cash flow analysis." (DeLisle and Griego 2008). So, if a project is feasible using the front-door analysis, it will likely be feasible under more sophisticated techniques as well.

The next two chapters further develop the concept of feasibility. In Chap. 7 we discuss why location is essential in real estate and extend the front-door analysis by making the location a choice variable. This will allow us to explore the feasibility of a project at any location within a city. We also develop a detailed numerical example that uses front-door analysis to show that it is difficult to make affordable housing projects work without subsidies or grants. In Chap. 8 we describe how federal and city subsidies such as Low-Income Housing Tax Credits and Tax Increment Financing can help make affordable housing projects feasible. The chapter stresses the importance of a more diverse capital structure since successful projects tend to use six to twelve sources of financing.

References

Ciochetti BA, Malizia E (2000) The application of financial analysis and market research to the real estate development process. In: DeLisle JR et al (eds) Essays in honor of James a. Graaskamp: ten years after. Springer, Boston, MA, pp 135–163

DeLisle J, Griego R (2008) Frontdoor/backdoor analysis. Case study. The University of Washington

Graaskamp JA (1972) A rational approach to feasibility analysis. Apprais J 40(October):513–521

Graaskamp JA (1981) Fundamentals of real estate development. The Urban Land Institute, Washington, DC

Malpezzi S (2015) The Wisconsin program in real estate and urban land economics: a century of tradition and innovation. University of Wisconsin, Madison, WI

Chapter 7
Location, Location, Location

Abstract In Chap. 6, we explained the concept of financial feasibility for a real estate development, described the front-door and back-door analyses in detail, and gave a simple example of each. One of the characteristics of the front-door analysis is that it only considers one specific location. However, housing could potentially be built in any place, and each site is different. How do we take account of the fact that building five miles from a city center is entirely different from building two miles from the city center? To address this question, this chapter extends the front-door analysis to make the location a choice variable, so that the model analyzes feasibility in any location. First, we briefly review the underlying economic model that describes how rents and land prices vary with location. Next, we develop a numerical example that will explore the feasibility of affordable housing development in multiple locations in a city. The model will show that it is incredibly challenging to make affordable housing "work" without subsidies or tax credits. In Chap. 8, we will continue building on the numerical example to show how subsidies can help make previously infeasible projects feasible.

There is a well-worn cliché that "real estate is about location, location, location".[1] There is undoubtedly some truth to this statement, most obviously because each piece of real estate is fixed to a specific location. While the value of a Da Vinci painting does not change much depending on where it is displayed, a house on the beach is much more valuable than an identical home located near a landfill. At the same time, the statement is not specific enough. What do we mean by location? Why is location so important for real estate? What makes some locations more desirable than others?

As James Graaskamp pointed out: "Location is often identified as the critical factor in a site, but it is seldom understood that location value is related to the

---

[1] The 1987 obituary of the British real estate tycoon Lord Harold Samuel credits him with coining the phrase "There are three things that matter in property: *location, location, location.*" However, a 1926 ad in the Chicago Tribune included the phrase "Attention salesmen, sales managers: *location, location, location,* close to Rogers Park." See William Safire. 6/29/2009. Location, Location, Location. *New York Times.*

© Springer Nature Switzerland AG 2019
J. P. Luque et al., *Affordable Housing Development,*
https://doi.org/10.1007/978-3-030-04064-2_7

functional needs of the activity and not the site." (Graaskamp 1981). In the case of housing, the functional needs include employment, schools, shopping, recreation, and others. The relationships between a household and other locations that serve the aforementioned functional needs are called linkages, and each requires the movement of people and goods. In turn, the costs of these movements are called "frictions", and households naturally try to minimize them. Therefore, locations that have the best linkages and reduce frictions will be more valuable. Put differently; we can define linkages as ties to the land with networks of supporting establishments and infrastructure which increase or decrease desirability of land or property. It is worth pointing out that crucial linkages vary depending on types of land use. For example, a law firm may value being close to their clients (i.e., in the central business district, with a concentration of jobs), while a manufacturing firm may value being close to a railroad or a major highway to save on shipping costs. Ultimately, locations with superior linkages will command higher land rents and prices.

More specifically, in describing the land rent patterns, we adopt the standard urban economics theory developed by Alonso, Mills, and Muth (Alonso 1960; Mills 1967; Muth 1969).[2] These models assume a monocentric city, where all employment is located in the city center, and roads extend radially from the center. Workers commute from various locations to the center. Thus, the critical linkage is employment, and people value being close to the center, where all the jobs are. In such a city, commuting costs are proportional to the distance from the center. If there are no differences in amenities at various locations, housing, and land rents will be the highest at the city center, and decline as one moves away from the center. This monocentric model of the city is elegant and intuitive. It was also a realistic description of most cities until the late nineteenth–early twentieth century.

With the invention of cars and large-scale construction of highways in the twentieth century, the rent patterns started to change. Since highways reduce travel time, locations near radial highways are more accessible, commanding higher rents. This resulted in rent gradient "ridges" around the major highways. Moreover, one or more "beltways" surround most modern cities. The effect of a beltway is similar to that of radial highways: a ring of higher rents forms around it. Finally, the intersections of radial highways and beltways also offer better accessibility. These intersections can form pockets where rent is even higher than along the radial highways. As a result, in modern cities rent is typically the highest in the center. It declines as one moves away from the center, but then increases within a specific range, before continuing to fall at longer distances. Figure 7.1 below shows an example of rent gradients with radial streets and with a beltway.

When the city only has radial streets, and no highways, commuting costs increase and rents decrease with distance. This is shown with the dashed line in the chart. When the city has faster roads, and in specific a beltway, commuting costs do not

---

[2] See also Casella (2001) for a more recent model of multiple mono-centric jurisdictions that provide local public goods to their residents. See also Dokow and Luque (2018) for an extension of Casella's model to the case of mixed-income jurisdictions.

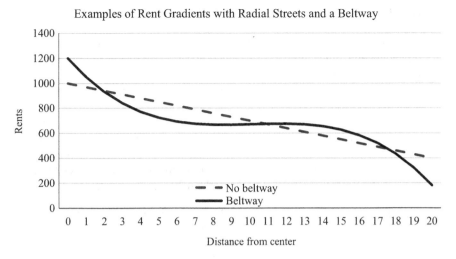

Fig. 7.1 In a city with only radial streets, the rent gradient is a downward-sloping straight line. If a city also has a beltway, rents may not strictly decline with distance from the CBD

always increase with distance. The solid line in the graph depicts the rent gradient in a city with a beltway. In this example, rents decline from the center to 9 miles, then slightly increase between 9 and 12 miles, before continuing to fall beyond 12 miles.

Numerical Example

The remainder of this chapter is dedicated to a mathematical model, which extends the front-door analysis to multiple locations, and shows how subsidies can bring the project into the feasibility region. We make the following definitions and assumptions for clarity:

- Properties' Net Operating Incomes are determined by market rents, vacancy rates, operating expense ratios, and project size (number of units). Market rents and vacancy rates may vary by location.
- Land prices depend on location. More desirable areas are more expensive than less desirable areas. Note that this does not mean that land prices always decline as one moves further and further away from city center. Standard reasons for a non-linear bid rent curve are access to amenities, access to public transportation, proximity to schools, and proximity to work centers.[3]
- In addition to land prices, we also allow for vacancy rates to vary based on location. Reasons justifying differences in vacancy rates across locations are

---

[3] See O'Sullivan (2012) for a baseline model to understand the bid rent curve.

access to local public goods, transportation nodes, and employment opportunities.
- For simplicity, we assume that labor, construction costs, and operating expenses do not depend on location. This assumption can be easily relaxed by considering the site and building characteristics.
- Total development cost is the sum of land cost, soft and hard construction costs, and the developer's fee.
- The building size, number of units, size of each unit, and quality of units are optimal at each location. In other words, the developer chooses the optimal combination of land and capital, which is dictated by their relative prices.
- The project is financially feasible if rents charged generate a Net Operating Income (NOI) that is sufficient to cover the debt service and equity dividends.

To make the example more concrete, suppose a residential developer is considering a multifamily development project for lower-income households, each of whom earns a monthly income of $1600 (200 hours per month at $8 per hour).[4] The project will have 100 identical apartments, every 1000 square feet. Construction costs are $7 million, regardless of location. The site cost varies with location. Employment is concentrated in the central business district (CBD), and land values are a function of distance from the CBD. The city extends 8 miles from the CBD in two directions: *East* and *West*. Each part of the city has its bid-rent curve. For the sake of presentation, we consider the following non-linear site cost functions for the apartment project in the two parts of the city:

$$Site\ Cost_{East} = \frac{\$5,000,000}{1+miles}$$

$$Site\ Cost_{West} = \frac{\$5,000,000}{1+miles} + 1,000,000 * miles$$

where "miles" represents the distance from the CBD in miles. We also consider non-linear vacancy rates, which depend on location, and are given by:

$$Vacancy\ Rate_{East} = \frac{7 * \sqrt{1+miles}}{200}$$

$$Vacancy\ Rate_{West} = \frac{7 * \sqrt{1+miles}}{100} - 0.02 * miles$$

---

[4] We use these numbers because (a) $8 is slightly above the Wisconsin minimum wage (which is $7.25) and (b) we chose 200 hours to highlight that this person is working more than full time (perhaps two jobs). Alternatively, 200 hours can be understood as two earners in a household, both working part time. The idea is that a single parent who earns above minimum wage and also works more that full time could still be rent burdened.

Numerical Example

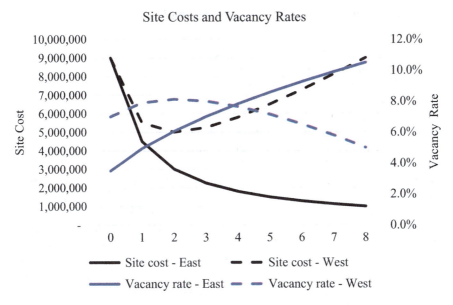

Fig. 7.2 Site costs and vacancy rates in the East and West

Site costs and vacancy rates as a function of distance from the center are shown in the Fig. 7.2 below. The chart shows that in the East, site costs decrease, and vacancy increases as one move away from the CBD. In the West, site costs lower, and vacancy rises only up to a certain distance from the center. After that, the changes occur in opposite directions.

Lenders are willing to finance up to 60% of the total development cost with a 25-year, 7% interest loan that requires annual payments, so the annual loan constant would be 0.0848. In the absence of any subsidies, the balance of the development budget comes from equity investors, who require an 8% annual return. Finally, the operating expenses are 25% of the effective gross income.

Given this information, we can conduct the extended front-door analysis, whereby minimum rents are calculated for any location in the city. Recall that the front-door analysis is a one-period financial feasibility model. This is in contrast to the traditional front-door analysis, where the minimum required rent for project feasibility is calculated for a specific site.

Development Is Unlikely Without Subsidies

Let us first consider feasibility in the absence of any government subsidies.[5] The required per unit rents for each part of the city are shown in the Tables 7.1 and 7.2 below. The tables also show the rent burden at each location, calculated as the ratio of household income to rent (academic researchers and policymakers usually define a household spending at least 30% of their income on rent as "rent burdened", and those spending at least 50% as "severely rent burdened").

In this case, it is highly unlikely that low-income residential development will be feasible in the West because all locations would require that households spend at least two-thirds of their income on rent. In contrast, the project may be viable in specific areas in the East. At locations 4–8 miles from the CBD, lower-income households would need to spend no more than 55% of their income on rent. As documented in Chap. 1, this is mostly the status quo in many large cities today. While development may strictly speaking be feasible, this scenario illustrates the affordability problem in a nutshell. Lower-income households would need to endure long commutes, with substantial monetary and time costs. Moreover, many households may not own cars and may need to use public transportation, which may not be available that far from the city center. For these reasons, state and local governments may (and do) encourage construction of lower-income housing closer to the CBD.

Conclusion

In this chapter, we discussed the importance of location in real estate development. The main contribution was to extend the front-door analysis to multiple locations. This allows a developer to explore feasibility at many locations simultaneously. The detailed numerical example of front-door analysis that we introduced showed the challenge of making affordable housing work in the absence of federal and local subsidies. In the next chapter we build on the same numerical example to incorporate two outstanding programs, one local (Tax Increment Financing) and the other federal (Low Income Housing Tax Credits). The example shows why subsidies are almost always needed to make affordable housing feasible.

---

[5]We extend the analysis to include subsidies in Chap. 9.

Table 7.1 Calculation of required rents for the East

East	Miles from the CBD								
	0	1	2	3	4	5	6	7	8
Site cost	9,000,000	4,500,000	3,000,000	2,250,000	1,800,000	1,500,000	1,285,714	1,125,000	1,000,000
Total development cost	16,000,000	11,500,000	10,000,000	9,250,000	8,800,000	8,500,000	8,285,714	8,125,000	8,000,000
Loan amount	9,600,000	6,900,000	6,000,000	5,550,000	5,280,000	5,100,000	4,971,429	4,875,000	4,800,000
Equity	6,400,000	4,600,000	4,000,000	3,700,000	3,520,000	3,400,000	3,314,286	3,250,000	3,200,000
Annual debt service	814,210	585,213	508,881	470,715	447,815	432,549	421,644	413,466	407,105
Required equity dividend	512,000	368,000	320,000	296,000	281,600	272,000	265,143	260,000	256,000
Required NOI	1,326,210	953,213	828,881	766,715	729,415	704,549	686,787	673,466	663,105
Effective gross income	1,768,280	1,270,951	1,105,175	1,022,287	972,554	939,398	915,716	897,954	884,140
Vacancy rate (%)	3.5	4.9	6.1	7.0	7.8	8.6	9.3	9.9	10.5
Required gross revenue	1,832,414	1,337,136	1,176,496	1,099,233	1,055,131	1,027,487	1,009,166	996,614	987,866
Required monthly rent/unit	**1527**	**1114**	**980**	**916**	**879**	**856**	**841**	**831**	**823**
Rent burden (%)	95	70	61	57	55	54	53	52	51

Table 7.2 Calculation of required rents for the West

West	Miles from the CBD								
	0	1	2	3	4	5	6	7	8
Site cost	9,000,000	5,500,000	5,000,000	5,250,000	5,800,000	6,500,000	7,285,714	8,125,000	9,000,000
Total development cost	16,000,000	12,500,000	12,000,000	12,250,000	12,800,000	13,500,000	14,285,714	15,125,000	16,000,000
Loan amount	9,600,000	7,500,000	7,200,000	7,350,000	7,680,000	8,100,000	8,571,429	9,075,000	9,600,000
Equity	6,400,000	5,000,000	4,800,000	4,900,000	5,120,000	5,400,000	5,714,286	6,050,000	6,400,000
Annual debt service	814,210	636,101	610,657	623,379	651,368	686,989	726,973	769,683	814,210
Required equity dividend	512,000	400,000	384,000	392,000	409,600	432,000	457,143	484,000	512,000
Required NOI	1,326,210	1,036,101	994,657	1,015,379	1,060,968	1,118,989	1,184,116	1,253,683	1,326,210
Effective gross income	1,768,280	1,381,468	1,326,210	1,353,839	1,414,624	1,491,986	1,578,821	1,671,577	1,768,280
Vacancy rate (%)	7.0	7.9	8.1	8.0	7.7	7.1	6.5	5.8	5.0
Required gross revenue	1,901,376	1,499,957	1,443,483	1,471,564	1,531,848	1,606,816	1,688,945	1,774,479	1,861,347
Required monthly rent/unit	**1584**	**1250**	**1203**	**1226**	**1277**	**1339**	**1407**	**1479**	**1551**
Rent burden (%)	99	78	75	77	80	84	88	92	97

References

Alonso W (1960) A theory of the urban land market. Pap Reg Sci 6(1):149–157
Casella A (2001) The role of market size in the formation of jurisdictions. Rev Econ Stud 68:83–108
Dokow E, Luque J (2018) Provision of local public goods in mixed income communities. J Hous Econ. https://doi.org/10.1016/j.jhe.2018.02.005 (in press)
Graaskamp J (1981) Fundamentals of real estate development. ULI Monograph
Mills ES (1967) An aggregative model of resource allocation in a metropolitan area. Am Econ Rev 57:197–210
Muth RF (1969) Cities and housing. University of Chicago Press, Chicago
O'Sullivan A (2012) Urban economics. McGraw-Hill/Irwin, Boston
Safire W (2009, June 29) Location, location, location. New York Times

Chapter 8
The Critical Role of TIF, LIHTC, and City Grants

Abstract This chapter introduces Tax Incremental Financing (TIF) and Low-Income Housing Tax Credits (LIHTC) in a financial feasibility model with heterogenous locations. We show that both TIF and LIHTC effectively allow landlords to charge lower rents and make housing more affordable.

The traditional real estate development process uses two primary sources of capital: equity and debt. However, in many metropolitan areas, the combination of prohibitive costs of development (most often due to high land prices) and lower rents often makes the development of affordable housing impossible without additional sources of capital. Properties typically do not generate sufficient income to cover the developer's costs and expected profits because of below-market rents. Consequently, much of new rental housing that has come online in the last 12 years has been targeted at the upper end of the market (Joint Center 2017). To make the construction of affordable housing feasible, private developers need to use various combinations of federal and local subsidies, tax increment financing, and grants, in addition to debt and equity. In this chapter, we examine how a more vibrant capital structure that includes Low Income Housing Tax Credits, Tax Increment Financing, and federal and local grants can make the development of affordable housing feasible. In doing so, we will further expand James Graaskamp's feasibility model by incorporating a more diverse capital structure.[1] We will use a stylized example to show how subsidies can turn previously impossible projects into a reality.[2] Less crucially, subsidies and grants also change the relative importance of both debt and equity. We will see that in well-structured deals the developer's equity can often be kept to a minimum.

In Chap. 6 we described Graaskamp's approach to feasibility, according to whom a project is feasible when "there is a reasonable likelihood of satisfying explicit

---

[1] Authors' conversations with industry professionals revealed that successful affordable housing projects often use funds from 6 to 12 different sources.

[2] For a more technical analysis to understand the role of LIHTC and TIF on affordable housing development using a general equilibrium framework, see Luque (2018).

objectives when a selected course of action is tested for fit to a context of specific constraints and limited resources." As someone who was well-trained both in academia and the industry, Graaskamp defined feasibility broadly: the project must meet not only the developer's objectives, but satisfy all parties involved, including lenders, regulators, and users. Chapter 6 also described how Graaskamp's front-door model could be used in feasibility studies, particularly when analyzing the suitability of a specific use for a site. Recall that this model starts with development costs and ends with the rent per square foot that makes the project feasible. The intermediate steps are: estimating the debt and equity amounts, calculating the corresponding debt service and equity dividend payments, and calculating the Net Operating Income (NOI) required for covering these debt and equity payments. If the rent per square foot is enough to generate such a NOI, we say that the project is feasible from a financial point of view.[3]

In Chap. 7 we extended the Graaskamp method by making the project's location a choice variable. While the traditional approach seeks to define the feasibility of development on a single site, our method described examines the possibility of development at any location. Locations, determined by the distance to the employment center, have different rents and vacancy rates. This allows the developer to use both the front-door and back-door models.

The high costs of development primarily due to high land prices, combined with lower rents, make the development of affordable housing infeasible in many metropolitan areas. As a result, much of new rental housing that has come online in the last 12 years has been targeted to the upper end of the market (Joint Center 2017). Therefore, government subsidies are often the difference between affordable housing being developed or not.

Financial Feasibility With and Without Subsidies

In Chap. 7, we developed a stylized example to examine economic viability of a rental housing development with only private sources of financing (debt and equity). Here, we extend the case to include private funding sources, as well as government subsidies such as TIF and LIHTC. There are three critical differences between development with and without subsidies. First, while subsidy programs (such as LIHTC, TIF, and various grants) vary widely in details and dollar amounts, to a

---

[3] *The front-door model* takes the site cost as a given when estimating the total development cost. But in practice site costs are often negotiable, and developers may be interested in knowing the maximum price they can pay for a site while keeping their project feasible. This question would be particularly relevant when the developer has a specific plan in mind and is searching for the appropriate location. In such cases, they may use *the back-door model*, which takes the prevailing market rents as a given, estimates the justified debt and equity amounts, adds these two to calculate the legitimate development costs, and finally "backs into" the maximum site cost that would justify the project.

developer, all these programs fundamentally have the same effect. They all reduce the capital budget by the amount of total subsidy.[4] In each case, the developer receives a lump-sum cash infusion at the start of the project. Second, the expected rental income (and therefore the value of the project) is lower if the developer decides to accept subsidies. Again, while specific requirements vary, most government subsidies put limits on the rent that can be charged, at least for some units. Typically, some of the units must be rented to lower-income households, who will pay no more than 30% of their income in rent. Third, cities usually subsidize projects only in specific areas, where the need for affordable housing is most significant. The effect is that the location choices will be more limited for developers who want to use subsidies.

These three conditions mean that government subsidies have two opposing effects. They encourage the construction of affordable housing units by making it cheaper. At the same time, they discourage it by reducing future rental income (and thus the value of the project) because of limits on rents and developers' location choices. In the example below, a developer who is considering an affordable housing project faces two choices: (1) where to build, and (2) whether to use government subsidies. Due to the cities' priorities, fewer locations are available if the developer uses subsidies.

Tax Increment Financing Usually Does Not Make or Break a Project

We next examine one mechanism by which cities incentivize housing construction—Tax Increment Financing (TIF). The new development will increase the site's value, leading to higher property taxes in the future. As described in detail in Chap. 4, the city estimates the difference between the current and future taxes (the tax increment), and issues bonds whose value is approximately equal to the present value of this increment. The proceeds from the bond issuance are given to the developer, which reduces total development cost. In this example, the city offers tax increment financing equal to 10% of total development cost to any lower-income housing project in the East, but not in the West. The city may have many reasons for preferring the East region, such as lack of affordable housing units, better availability of public transportation, and others. The results from the extended front-door analysis, as well as rent burdens for the two areas, are shown in Tables 8.1 and 8.2.

Since there are no cost reductions, feasibility does not improve in the West. It does improve slightly in the East—the rent burden is less than 55% within 2 miles of

---

[4]While LIHTC does not require the developer to make any payments in the future, TIF stipulates that future property tax payments will be used to service the debt issued to finance the project. However, from the developer's point of view TIF can also be considered a free cash infusion, because the developer would have to pay the higher property taxes in the future even without TIF.

Table 8.1 Calculation of required rents for the East with TIF

	East—10% TIF			Miles from the CBD					
	0	1	2	3	4	5	6	7	8
Site cost	9,000,000	4,500,000	3000,000	2,250,000	1,800,000	1,500,000	1,285,714	1,125,000	1000,000
Total development cost	16,000,000	11,500,000	10,000,000	9,250,000	8,800,000	8,500,000	8,285,714	8,125,000	8,000,000
TIF—East	1,600,000	1,150,000	1000,000	925,000	880,000	850,000	828,571	812,500	800,000
Loan amount	9,600,000	6,900,000	6,000,000	5,550,000	5,280,000	5,100,000	4,971,429	4,875,000	4,800,000
Equity	4,800,000	3,450,000	3000,000	2,775,000	2,640,000	2,550,000	2,485,714	2,437,500	2,400,000
Annual debt service	814,210	585,213	508,881	470,715	447,815	432,549	421,644	413,466	407,105
Req. equity dividend	384,000	276,000	240,000	222,000	211,200	204,000	198,857	195,000	192,000
Required NOI	1,198,210	861,213	748,881	692,715	659,015	636,549	620,501	608,466	599,105
Effective gross income	1,597,613	1,148,284	998,508	923,620	878,687	848,732	827,335	811,288	798,806
Vacancy rate	4%	5%	6%	7%	8%	9%	9%	10%	11%
Required gross revenue	1,655,557	1,208,081	1,062,946	993,140	953,294	928,319	911,766	900,425	892,521
Required monthly rent/unit	**1380**	**1007**	**886**	**828**	**794**	**774**	**760**	**750**	**744**
Rent burden	86%	63%	55%	52%	50%	48%	47%	47%	46%

Table 8.2 Calculation of required rents for the West with TIF

	West—No TIF			Miles from the CBD					
	0	1	2	3	4	5	6	7	8
Site cost	9,000,000	5,500,000	5000,000	5,250,000	5,800,000	6,500,000	7,285,714	8,125,000	9,000,000
Total development cost	16,000,000	12,500,000	12,000,000	12,250,000	12,800,000	13,500,000	14,285,714	15,125,000	16,000,000
No TIF—West	–	–	–	–	–	–	–	–	–
Loan amount	9,600,000	7,500,000	7,200,000	7,350,000	7,680,000	8,100,000	8,571,429	9,075,000	9,600,000
Equity	6,400,000	5000,000	4,800,000	4,900,000	5,120,000	5,400,000	5,714,286	6,050,000	6,400,000
Annual debt service	814,210	636,101	610,657	623,379	651,368	686,989	726,973	769,683	814,210
Req. equity dividend	512,000	400,000	384,000	392,000	409,600	432,000	457,143	484,000	512,000
Required NOI	1,326,210	1,036,101	994,657	1,015,379	1,060,968	1,118,989	1,184,116	1,253,683	1,326,210
Effective gross income	1,768,280	1,381,468	1,326,210	1,353,839	1,414,624	1,491,986	1,578,821	1,671,577	1,768,280
Vacancy rate	7%	8%	8%	8%	8%	7%	7%	6%	5%
Required gross revenue	1,901,376	1,499,957	1,443,483	1,471,564	1,531,848	1,606,816	1,688,945	1,774,479	1,861,347
Required monthly rent/unit	**1584**	**1250**	**1203**	**1226**	**1277**	**1339**	**1407**	**1479**	**1551**
Rent burden	99%	78%	75%	77%	80%	84%	88%	92%	97%

the CBD. Households spend less than half their income on rent if the project is built 4–8 miles from the CBD.

Low-Income Housing Tax Credit Can Make a Huge Difference

Finally, we consider another common subsidy: The Low-Income Housing Tax Credit (LIHTC). In this example, the project receives LIHTC equal to 40% of development cost, in addition to the 10% TIF financing. Again, both are available for projects built in the East, but not in the West. Each state's housing authority allocates LIHTC by a competitive process, using a formal scoring system, as we described in Chap. 3. Typically, a substantial share of the score depends on things like access to jobs, public transit, and amenities, all of which vary by location.

As with TIF, the effect of LIHTC is to reduce the overall cost of the project, meaning a smaller loan and no equity would be needed for projects in the East. One notable difference between the two programs is that LIHTC requires that: (1) a certain proportion of units must be rented to lower-income households, and (2) rent cannot exceed 30% of the tenant's income. Notice that if the project is built in the East, the combination of LIHTC, TIF, and debt cover 100% of the development cost, meaning the developer does not contribute any equity. Tables 8.3 and 8.4 contain a row showing this rent cap, based on the monthly household income of $1600.

Lower-income housing development is still infeasible in the West since subsidies are not available there. In the East, projects are feasible across more locations. Rent burden is below 50% at all sites, and lower-income households spend less than 30% of their income on rent 3 miles away from the CBD.

The chart in Fig. 8.1 shows the rent burdens under the various scenarios described above. Little affordable housing would be built in the absence of subsidies—the top two rent burden lines never fall below 50%. If affordability is defined as a rent burden of 30% or less, then both TIF and LIHTC are needed to make development feasible. In this case, lower-income housing could be built on sites 3 to 8 miles from the CBD. If the government defines affordability as rent burden of 50% or less, then only TIF may be sufficient, and LIHTC is unnecessary. When only TIF is used, the lower-income housing can be built 4 miles away from the CBD or further.

In the example above, we assumed that rent of all units would be capped at 30% of the tenant's income. In practice, at least some units would be rented at prevailing market rents. Recall that the minimum legal requirement for LIHTC funding is that either: (a) at least 20% of units must be leased to households earning no more than 50% of county median income (CMI), or (b) at least 40% of units must be rented to households earning no more than 60% of CMI. Furthermore, rent cannot exceed 30% of the maximum eligible income for the area. Thus, it appears that the developer should limit the number of units with below-market rents to an absolute minimum.

Table 8.3 Calculation of required rents for the East with LIHTC

	East – 10% TIF and 40% LIHTC			Miles from the CBD					
	0	1	2	3	4	5	6	7	8
Site cost	9,000,000	4,500,000	3000,000	2,250,000	1,800,000	1,500,000	1,285,714	1,125,000	1000,000
Total development cost	16,000,000	11,500,000	10,000,000	9,250,000	8,800,000	8,500,000	8,285,714	8,125,000	8,000,000
LIHTC—East	6,400,000	4,600,000	4,000,000	3,700,000	3,520,000	3,400,000	3,314,286	3,250,000	3,200,000
TIF—East	1,600,000	1,150,000	1000,000	925,000	880,000	850,000	828,571	812,500	800,000
Loan amount	8,000,000	5,750,000	5000,000	4,625,000	4,400,000	4,250,000	4,142,857	4,062,500	4,000,000
Equity	–	–	–	–	–	–	–	–	–
Annual debt service	678,508	487,678	424,068	392,262	373,179	360,457	351,370	344,555	339,254
Required equity dividend	–	–	–	–	–	–	–	–	–
Required NOI	678,508	487,678	424,068	392,262	373,179	360,457	351,370	344,555	339,254
Effective gross income	904,677	650,237	565,423	523,017	497,573	480,610	468,494	459,406	452,339
Vacancy rate	4%	5%	6%	7%	8%	9%	9%	10%	11%
Required gross revenue	937,490	684,098	601,912	562,383	539,820	525,677	516,304	509,882	505,406
Required monthly rent/unit	**781**	**570**	**502**	**469**	**450**	**438**	**430**	**425**	**421**
Rent cap (30% of income)	480	480	480	480	480	480	480	480	480
Rent burden	49%	36%	31%	29%	28%	27%	27%	27%	26%

Table 8.4 Calculation of required rents for the West with LIHTC

	East—No TIF, No LIHTC			Miles from the CBD					
	0	1	2	3	4	5	6	7	8
Site cost	9,000,000	5,500,000	5000,000	5,250,000	5,800,000	6,500,000	7,285,714	8,125,000	9,000,000
Construction cost	7,000,000	7,000,000	7,000,000	7,000,000	7,000,000	7,000,000	7,000,000	7,000,000	7,000,000
Total development cost	16,000,000	12,500,000	12,000,000	12,250,000	12,800,000	13,500,000	14,285,714	15,125,000	16,000,000
No LIHTC—West	–	–	–	–	–	–	–	–	–
No TIF—West	–	–	–	–	–	–	–	–	–
Loan amount	8,000,000	6,250,000	6,000,000	6,125,000	6,400,000	6,750,000	7,142,857	7,562,500	8,000,000
Equity	8,000,000	6,250,000	6,000,000	6,125,000	6,400,000	6,750,000	7,142,857	7,562,500	8,000,000
Annual debt service	678,508	530,084	508,881	519,483	542,806	572,491	605,811	641,402	678,508
Required equity dividend	640,000	500,000	480,000	490,000	512,000	540,000	571,429	605,000	640,000
Required NOI	1,318,508	1,030,084	988,881	1,009,483	1,054,806	1,112,491	1,177,239	1,246,402	1,318,508
Effective Gross Income	1,758,011	1,373,446	1,318,508	1,345,977	1,406,409	1,483,322	1,569,652	1,661,869	1,758,011
Vacancy rate	7%	8%	8%	8%	8%	7%	7%	6%	5%
Required Gross Revenue	1,890,334	1,491,247	1,435,101	1,463,018	1,522,952	1,597,485	1,679,136	1,764,174	1,850,538
Required monthly rent/unit	**1575**	**1243**	**1196**	**1219**	**1269**	**1331**	**1399**	**1470**	**1542**
Rent cap (30% of income)	480	480	480	480	480	480	480	480	480
Rent burden	98%	78%	75%	76%	79%	83%	87%	92%	96%

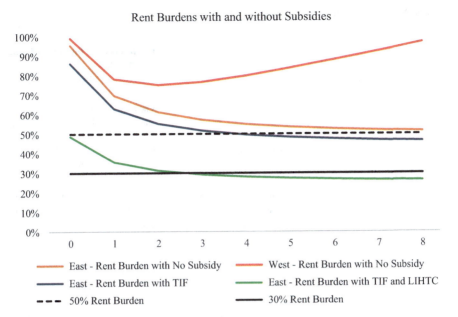

Fig. 8.1 Construction of affordable housing is infeasible in the West, which does not receive any subsidies. In the East, subsidies make the creation of affordable units feasible at certain locations

This is not the case in practice. Data show that an overwhelming majority of units in affordable housing projects that use LIHTC are below-market units. The reason is simple: the amount of tax credits (the subsidy) available to the developer increases with the number of below-market rent units. Therefore, the developer faces a tradeoff. For each below-market rent unit, they give up the difference between market rent and the actual rent charged and gains additional tax credits. The optimal combination of market rent and below-market rent units will depend on this tradeoff. For instance, if the market rent is much higher than the rent capped by CMI (as would be the case in comparatively expensive housing markets), then the developer has an incentive to keep the number of below-market units to a minimum. If on the other hand, the market rent is not much higher than rent capped by CMI (as in comparatively cheap housing markets), then the developer does not gain much from having a lot of units with market rent. In this case, they would choose to maximize their tax credits by offering most (or even all) units at below-market rent, although the plan would still likely want to include provisions to have a series of several types of rents, such as a portion at 50% CMI, a portion at 30% CMI, and a portion of the housing development to assist homeless populations.

Table 8.5 Model of development costs, part 1

Spatial feasibility analysis				
		Formulas used for site cost and vacancy rate:		
Location: Miles from CBD	6	Site cost	45,000/ (1 + miles from CBD)	
		Vacancy rate	7.071 *((1 + miles from CBD))^(1/2)/ 200	
	Site acquisition cost	$6429	/ unit	$385,714
Square feet				
60,000	Residential area hard cost per SF	$130.00	/sf	$7,800,000
12,000	Common area hard cost per SF	$95.00		$1,140,000
0	Commercial area hard cost per SF	$75.00	/sf	–
72,000				$8,940,000
Unit #'s	# of underground parking stalls	60		
60	Cost per underground parking stall	$15,000	/ stall	$900,000
	Appliances/Furniture/Equipment	$5000	unit	$300,000
Square feet	Soft cost as a percent of total hard cost	10%		$1,014,000
1000				
	Construction budget			$10,854,000
Efficiency				
20%	Developer fee	12%		$1,302,480
Tax credit rate	**Total development cost**			**$12,542,194**
85%	Less: City Contribution (% of cost)	0.00%		0
	Less: Tax Credit Equity (% of units)	0.00%		0
	Net development cost			**$12,542,194**

A Financial Feasibility Model with TIF, LIHTC and City Subsidies

We conclude the chapter with another, more comprehensive and realistic model of feasibility that incorporates TIF, LIHTC, and city subsidies as part of the capital stack. The first part of the model estimates the total development cost. The difference between this model and the one we used in earlier examples in Chaps. 6, 7 and 8 is that this model looks at development cost in much more detail.[5] Also, the numbers used here are quite realistic for a mid-sized Midwestern city like Madison, Wisconsin. Table 8.5 shows this first part of the model.

---

[5]We thank our colleague Tom Landgraf for developing and sharing this model.

Table 8.6 Calculation of debt service

Debt calculation	
Loan to cost ratio	80%
Mortgage loan	$ 10,033,755
Loan fee	1.25%
Loan rate	5%
Loan term	25 years
Debt service	**$703,876/year**

The table shows the estimation of the total and net development costs for a hypothetical 60-unit multi-family housing project, which is located 6 miles from the CBD. Following the discussion in Chap. 7, both site cost per unit and vacancy rate depend on location and are calculated based on the formulas in the top-right cells highlighted in pink. Note that all cells highlighted in green are input cells—we could change these numbers based on data or assumptions.

This project consists of 60 apartments, with 1000 square feet each, and 12,000 square feet non-leasable in common areas. There is no commercial space—this project is entirely residential. The 20% efficiency number in the table represents the ratio of common areas (12,000 SF) to the total area (72,000 SF). The 85% tax credit rate represents the expectation that the LIHTC credit (if available) will cover 85% of the total development cost. The rest of the cost numbers are all realistic estimates of current construction costs. For example, note that the construction cost per square foot is lower for common areas than for residential areas.

The last two items to note in the table are city contribution (% of cost) and tax credit equity (% of unity). These items are subsidies from local and federal governments, which if granted, would reduce the overall development cost. Thus, "net development cost" in the table is simply "total development cost" less city contribution and tax credit equity. Note that in this base version of the model, we are assuming both items are set to zero—there are no subsidies. Later we will explain how such subsidies can reduce the rent per unit that would make the project feasible.

Next, we move to the calculation of debt and equity needed to fund the project. First, lenders will offer a loan based on a maximum loan-to-cost ratio and the total development budget. We show this calculation in Table 8.6

In this case, lenders are willing to fund up to 80% of the $12.54 million net development cost, with a loan fee of 1.25%, 5% interest rate, and a 25-year term, with monthly payments. This gives us the maximum loan amount of $10,033,755, and annual debt service of $703,876. The mortgage payments are only based on the loan amount, interest rate, and the term. In other words, the loan fee cannot be financed and becomes part of the equity required. As before, notice that all cells highlighted in green are input cells.

With the traditional front-door analysis, the required equity is merely the part of the development cost that the loan will not cover. In the case of affordable housing, there is a possibility that the city may use Tax Increment Financing, as described in Chap. 4. If the project does receive TIF funding, then the equity required would be reduced by that amount. This is shown in Table 8.7.

Table 8.7 Calculation of required equity dividend

Equity calculation	
Gross cash equity required	$2,633,861
Tax increment financing	
Net cash equity required	$2,633,861
Equity dividend rate	8%
Required equity dividend	**$210,709**

Table 8.8 Calculation of required gross revenue service

Required rent calculation							
Net operating income							$914,585
			100%				
Net leasable area	Residential	60,000	sf				
	Commercial	–	sf				
Operating expenses	Residential	$3000	PUPY			$180,000	
	Commercial	$3.75	/sf/year			–	
				Building value			
Property tax	CAP rate	5.00%		$12,528,560			
	Tax rate	2.30%		$4803		$288,157	
		7.30%					
Required effective gross income							$1,382,742
Vacancy loss	Vacancy rate	9.35%					$129,342
Required gross revenue				$25,201	Unit annual	$1,512,084/year	
				$25.201	psf/annual		

The table shows that once the mortgage covers the first $10,033,755 of the $12.54 million development cost, the remaining $2,633,861 must be covered by equity. Note that this also includes the loan fee, which is assumed to be 1.5% of the loan amount. If there is any TIF forthcoming, then the net cash equity required would be reduced by that amount. In this example, we are assuming there is no TIF funding available. Given the equity dividend rate of 8%, the required equity dividend is $210,709. The sum of this necessary equity dividend and annual debt service give us the minimum Net Operating Income (NOI) that the project must generate to make it feasible. From this NOI, we can calculate the required gross revenue and rent per unit. These series of calculations are shown in Table 8.8.

Conclusion

As we have established, debt investors (lenders) require an annual debt service of $703,876, while equity investors (owners) require an annual equity dividend of $210,709. This means that to provide minimum returns for the two main sources of funds, the project must produce at least $914,585 in net operating income.

We assume that operating expenses are $3000 per unit per year or $180,000 per year for the entire property. The next major expense is property taxes, which are based on the value of the property. This is calculated by dividing the NOI by the appropriate capitalization ratio (cap rate), which in this example is assumed to be 5%. This dividing $914,585 by 5% gives us the property value of $12,528,560. Multiplying this by the property tax rate of 2.3% results in the annual property tax bill of $1,382,742. Adding operating expenses and property tax gives us the required effective gross income.

The final adjustment is for expected vacancy loss. In this example, the vacancy rate is assumed to be high at 9.35% of the effective gross income. Adding the $129,342 to the effective gross income gives us $1,512,084, which is the required annual gross revenue that would make the project feasible. In other words, given this location and particular funding sources, this project would only be feasible if the rent per unit were at least $25,200 ($1,512,084/60) per year or $2100 per month.

This is relatively high rent, particularly for a location that is 6 miles from the CBD. Using the 30% rent-to-income threshold, only households with annual incomes exceeding $84,000 could comfortably afford these units. For low-income households, these apartments are entirely unaffordable. As we argued earlier in this chapter, the solution is to reduce the net development cost by injecting city grants/subsidies and LIHTC funds. This would have the effect of lower debt and equity requirements, which in turn would reduce the NOI and rent required. Furthermore, given how expensive rents are, the subsidies would need to be substantial, around 40–50% of the total development budget.

Conclusion

In this chapter, we developed a financial feasibility model with heterogeneous locations that also incorporates Tax Incremental Financing (TIF) and Low-Income Housing Tax Credits (LIHTC). While the conclusions depend on the assumptions made, the more significant lesson is that affordable housing is rarely feasible without some sort of federal, or local subsidies and grants, particularly in the expensive markets. In the next chapter, we dig deeper into the financing of affordable housing. Due to the sheer number and complexities of federal, state, and local subsidies and programs that can be used to finance such projects, many developers (particularly those who are just starting out in the industry) tend not the have the institutional knowledge, expertise, or resources required to make practical use of them. In many cases, they ask other public, private, and non-profit organizations for help. For example, when a development company receives Low Income Housing Tax Credits, it needs to sell these credits to investors, which is a lengthy and costly process. In such cases, organizations that specialize in syndicating credits can provide a valuable service. Chapter 9 will discuss an example of an organization that provides syndication and other related services to developers.

References

Joint Center for Housing Studies of Harvard University (2017) The State of the Nation's Housing: Harvard University

Luque J (2018) Assessing the role of TIF and LIHTC in an equilibrium model of affordable housing development. Reg Sci Urban Econ. Available online at https://doi.org/10.1016/j.regsciurbeco.2018.06.005. Accessed 6 July 2018

Chapter 9
Affordable Housing Development: Further Considerations for Developers

Abstract In this chapter, we cover the perspective of the public, private, and non-profit aspects of lending and financing for the affordable housing market. In particular, we will focus on Community Development Finance Institutions (CDFI), using Cinnaire Lending as an example. Such organizations fill a vital niche in the process of affordable housing development, offering services that banks and other traditional lenders do not. For example, they provide predevelopment loans that can be used for standard costs incurred with third-party vendors such as market studies, architectural plans, and legal fees. They can also offer short-term acquisition loans to acquire affordable housing properties.

Why Non-profit Lenders Are Needed

To explain the institutional details of our discussion of the private sector, we must understand that the public political debate in the United States does not often focus on the issue of housing. Only once in several decades is there a significant market-changing federal shift in policy. Still, since the last meaningful reform of the national policy impacting the housing market happened in 1986, it is not unreasonable to expect that we are on the cusp of another federal level shift. As we write this in early 2018, there are national level proposals to do away with some past credits and cut HOME funds. However, the market will not be able to fill this gap. If those funds are reduced, the creation of new subsidies would be necessary to sustain the same level of federal support for affordable housing. Additionally, there are substantial differences from state to state. For instance, Minnesota has good comparative rates for subsidies, when set side by side with Wisconsin. It has good transit-oriented development funds, more soft funds to be used as grants, more non-profit service organizations, and more bond resources that it has developed to affordable housing development over the course of the past decade.

The biggest challenge at present is that without an *increase* in Section 8, Section 42 and HUD funds, these programs are essentially facing a de facto *cut*, even if they are kept at present levels, as housing costs continue to increase. The affordable housing market, hence, is overburdened. This creates a distinct need for financing mixed-income units, which many non-profit developers are particularly interested in developing. The next most significant challenge is then developing a project that a lender will find attractive. If the development was 50 units, for example, most would go at 40% and 50% CMI; keeping in mind that 50–60% CMI rent is still between $800 and $900/month. This would only leave a small number of units for 30% CMI (e.g., ten units), with a lower number (e.g., 5–6 units) being set aside for high-need tenants or service housing for formerly homeless individuals. What this means for the individuals living in those units is that, if they are just living on Social Security Income (SSI), which averages at just around $750/month for an individual, they are only going to be able to afford the 30% CMI units or less. The need for affordable housing is apparent.

Given that an affordable housing development plan requires a robust capital stack, it is foreseeable that developers will have to work with some form of financing to establish a feasible financial plan. Many public and private lenders are involved in financing development projects. However, it is vital to consider non-profit lenders who work directly with affordable housing development, because of their expert understanding of the market niche, as well as their commitment to working with communities in need. An example is Cinnaire Lending Corporation, which is a certified Community Development Financial Institution[1] (CDFI), serving nine states in the mid-Atlantic and Great Lakes regions. Headquartered in Lansing, MI, Cinnaire runs its Wisconsin operations through its Madison office.

An Example of a Non-profit Lender

What does a non-profit lender offer that a for-profit lender cannot? Before we answer this question, we should clarify that the most common position holds that both profit and non-profit lenders are needed in a balanced marketplace. Non-profit lenders will have conditions established with each of the needs of their organizations. For example, Cinnaire does not do any construction financing. However, they can help with providing reasonable assessments of proposals, through discussing what they might and might not cover, and what might be reasonable, such as estimating that if they were going to cover the permanent loan for a long-term project, suggesting the amount of the private loan needed. This would invite the developer to seek other potential private lenders, to gather their interest in the development. From the perspective of the non-profit lender, this is good, because having more lenders at the table attracts more attention to affordable housing development and provides more capital for the sector. Furthermore, the attention

---

[1] According to the Opportunity Finance Network, the leading national network of CDFIs, "Community development financial institutions (CDFIs) are private financial institutions that are 100% dedicated to delivering responsible, affordable lending to help low-income, low-wealth, and other disadvantaged people and communities join the economic mainstream." See https://ofn.org/what-cdfi

might bring in the interest of a foundation, which could make a grant. An example of such a foundation would be the Hellen Bader Foundation (Milwaukee), which focuses on workforce development, youth, and older adults. Other foundations have been particularly active in cities such as Detroit, Michigan. For example, JPMorgan Chase has been active with CDFIs in Detroit.

By combining the work of a granting agency, TIF, LIHTC, and other sources, a development project would begin to look more viable for a permanent lender. Ideally, a non-profit like Cinnaire would see this as an opportunity for a permanent loan. Developers who come to start a conversation with Cinnaire are usually experienced or have partnered with someone with significant LIHTC experience. Cinnaire views experience favorably since expertise is one of the scoring fields for LIHTC applications in most states (see Chap. 3). Non-profit lenders like Cinnaire generally want to examine a proposed budget and pro forma income statement that maps out 15 years of financial projections, the length of the compliance period of tax credits. In some situations, there is enough equity and soft funding, and there is no permanent debt. More typically, there are fees associated with the municipality, a deferred developer's fee paid from cash flow, and most syndicators will not want to leave an agreement, as the result of a buyout proposal, before year 12 or 13. This could get problematic on the tax credit side of matters. The non-profit lender is in the circumstance for the long-term, so they are going to want to have an idea of how the developer will balance the finances long term to avoid any such difficulties.

Non-profit lenders will occasionally finance pre-development loans, although much of the financing is done at the post-LIHTC preservation stage. Often the pre-development loan would go toward aspects of architectural fees, engineering plans, and LIHTC application fees (keeping in mind that there are multiple rounds of costs). These pre-development loans are sometimes used for site acquisition, so it is essential to keep in mind that alternative funds may have to be secured for site acquisition. Even still, a pre-development loan could be quite significant, between $250,000 and $300,000. However, the hope with this process, from the perspective of the non-profit lender, would be to establish a relationship with the developer that leads to them working through the process of covering the equity syndication or the permanent loan for the project. These loans are typically for 15 to 18 year terms with a 30 or 35 year amortization. The equity syndication process would pool a collection of deals from individual developers. While many larger banks would require that the equity syndicator receive a benefit fee, in addition to the target return that would go to the investors that enter the deal, a non-profit syndicator may be more open to flexible fees.

Banks have had incentives to reinvest in the communities that they operate in since the Community Reinvestment Act (CRA 1977) went into effect. They are judged on lending, investing, and community service, and have oversight boards that look into their compliance with these measures. These compliance measures generate tax benefits and CRA credit for the financial institution. In this case, associated investors will get skittish about assessing the rents for commercial and market rate residential spaces, since those markets are highly flexible, but they are more interested in affordable housing markets because the demands of those markets are much more consistent. Non-profit lenders do well in this environment, and they tend to apply many best practices common in real estate lending. Pre-development financing is another opportunity for non-profit lenders to serve their clients.

Today's market for equity is quite competitive. However, the requirements for the guarantor strength and the standards for maintaining funds tightened after the recession. The current operating deficit guarantee for a project could be as much as half a million dollars, while the guarantee on a construction loan could be as much as 6 or 7 million dollars (the full amount of the loan), although we should note that this is not a dollar-for-dollar equity amount. Instead, it is based on an assessment of total assets and liquidity. Construction sites that require cleaning, serious repair of existing damaged structures, or clean-ups of environmental hazards can cause severe overruns in a project, leaving the lending agency to ask how a developer will cover for these potential expenses. Overruns often come out of the calculation of the developer's fee, so it is crucial for them to cover the project well. With these factors in mind, it is fair for a developer to presuppose that they will need to keep half a million of liquid capital on hand, not used for the development, but to hold in reserves. This money should not be used for the project at all, however. For example, in the case of a pre-development loan, the half million should be kept in reserves, while 10% of the loan amount is put forward by the developer, and another 90% is put together by the lender. The capital flow is then used to gather other sources of cash flow, and the calculations and ratios of payment are adjusted as the project moves forward. Typically, equity will ultimately come from other sources, and the developer will need to have an operating reserve for the project at an estimated rate of 6 months of operating expenses and principal and interest payments. In a model deal (for example a 9% LIHTC deal), the equity coming from investors in the project will be 60 to 70%, and the amount of must-pay permanent debt depends on the cash flow of the project, and what the cash flow of the project can support.

Going Deeper: Cinnaire as an Example of a Lender

As mentioned, Cinnnaire works regionally across the mid-Atlantic (except for the State of New York) and upper Midwest regions in the United States. Their mission is to contribute toward community development. For example, they cover permanent loans for LIHTC projects, cover pre-financing for the projects, and might be willing, depending on the plan, to cover the possibility of acquisition financing in some circumstances. The non-profit started in Michigan and then rapidly expanded to surrounding states. They put together pools of tax credit investors matched with a pool of housing developments as a financing specialty. Their niche role in the financial market is networking between investors and developers, to cover the long-term finances of development projects.

An essential factor in their program is the Community Reinvestment Act (CRA 1977), which maintains that lending agencies and banks should be doing some good in the communities they are working in. The CRA, therefore, includes a service test and many banks use the affordable housing market as a primary target to fulfill their CRA obligations. Despite these requirements, the market for affordable housing financing through the LIHTC program temporarily dipped during the 2007–2009 recession, because large corporations were taking losses, and hence did not need to purchase the tax credits. More recent changes were also introduced into the market after the 2016 election. Pricing for equity dropped quickly after the election in anticipation of lower corporate income tax rates to be proposed by the Republican-controlled Congress. Indeed, the Tax Cuts and Jobs Act of 2017 reduced the top marginal corporate income tax rate to 21%, which will no doubt make purchases of LIHTC credits less attractive.

Despite, or perhaps because of, the market uncertainty, developers will have to expect to build and maintain relationships with Community Development Financial Institutions (CDFIs), as these organizations fill gaps in the financial market that aren't covered by banks. CDFIs vary in nature, and each organization has a different sort of market feel to their coverage. For example, the Midwest portion of Cinnaire has traditionally focused more on the equity side of their financial market. It provides pre-development loans, short-term loans, permanent mortgage loans, and community facility financing.

Cinnaire targets deals for which it will be syndicating credits and/or providing permanent debt because of the long-term payoffs for its programs as investors, which gives it more capital for continuing to finance community development targeted at affordable housing reliably. Meanwhile, Cinnaire's predevelopment loans can be used to cover many expenses, such as standard costs incurred with third-party vendors, such as market studies, architectural plans, and legal costs. Predevelopment loans are presented to and approved by Cinnaire's Loan Committee. The loans are typically unsecured, with terms typically ranges from 6 to 18 months. Loans can range from $25,000 to $500,000, and the typical size is $250,000. It is important to remember that predevelopment loans get paid off by the date of closing. Next, their acquisition loans are of a different nature. Cinnaire targets deals, which it will be syndicating credits and/or providing permanent debts. Cinnaire has a loan term of up to 24 months to acquire affordable housing properties; quarterly interest payments are required. Cinnaire sometimes uses grants to fund predevelopment and acquisition loans, in that grant funding can be used if specific requirements of the associated grant are met.

Cinnaire's primary financial product is the *Immediate Loan Product*, and it is a Fannie Mae approved lender for these products. The immediate loan product is a permanent loan. This is predominantly a refinance structure, one used for an existing property—although occasionally through bridging its own equity—it has used the Fannie Mae product on 9% LIHTC deals. They are used for properties that are currently operating and can demonstrate the ability to pay debt service. Properties need to submit 2 years of operational and occupancy history for review and sizing for the loan. All properties undergoing rehabilitation are eligible if residents are not displaced. They also have much longer loan terms. Various loan terms are available, although they are typically 15 to 18 years in their most popular form, with a minimum debt service coverage ratio of 1.15. These loans can be structured up to 90% (with new credits) loan to value; 80% loan to value for refinanced deals.

Permanent loans, however, are also subject to the stability of the long-term market. Hence, an essential factor in their relatively increasing stability has been the improvements in financing construction costs. In short, construction financing has become more comfortable, making developments more viable in the long-term. But they are also impacted by other long-term market structures. For example, the 2007–2009 recession caused many development deals to fall through. Normally the investors who are limited partners, contribute equity in installments, or "draws". The first installment may be for 15% and is provided before construction commences. However, leading up to the recession, the housing market was "hot", and many deals involved an initial installment of only 5%. When the recession hit, and house prices collapsed, some investors "limited partners" were unable or unwilling to extend any future installments beyond the initial 5%. This was primarily because investors started suffering losses, making tax credits useless. As a result, many projects were abandoned. The American Recovery and Reinvestment Act of 2009 (ARRA) did help a lot of deals get completed in the long run—since the agreements no longer needed the external equity investors.

Cinnaire's second most common financial product is an *Unfunded Forward Commitment Loan Product,* which is also a permanent loan. They are to be used with properties that have a separate construction loan. The commitment can run from 6 to 30 months. They have a debt service coverage ratio minimum of 1.15, loan to value ratio of 90%, and 1% origination fee. They have a 2% refundable deposit required, which is repaid after the property's NOI stabilizes. Their current legal fees are fixed at $12,500. The borrower also must pay for an appraisal, Phase I Environmental checks, title, survey, flood certification, and capital needs assessment if the project is an acquisition rehab, which could total up to $50,000. Plan and cost review will also be required prior to rate lock. These reports are often engaged by multiple parties and shared.

The unfunded forward commitment loan differs from construction funds, which are only designed to get through the construction and lease-up phase. They also differ from a permanent loan that stretches over the entire 30-year compliance period, and perhaps beyond. Some lenders who offer both construction and permanent loans can sometimes structure a loan as a construction-permanent loan as well, with an "A" loan and a "B" loan. The "A loan" will typically be for the amount of the long-term permanent loan, but will come in during construction. It will have an interest-only period when no payments are required, as well as a period when the loan is amortized and debt service payments are required. The "B loan" will be a construction bridge loan only, intended to bridge some of the equity payments that come in at completion and stabilization later in the process. Once the construction is completed, a permanent loan is used to pay back the construction loan.

In all cases, the lender will plan to ask: *What are typical items that are seen in soft costs?* They will encompass the market study—Phase II engineering reports, consultants, developer fee, operating reserve, accounting, and legal. The developer will pay the origination fees to the lender. A construction inspector, who will do plans and monthly visits, will also need to be paid. In a 50-unit deal—minus developing fee and operating reserve taken out—$600,000–700,000 could be an acceptable amount to expect to pay for this particular phase of the project.

Typically, a developer should expect that the construction loan, city grants, and local municipal grants to be at least part of the outside financial providers for a project. Construction loans might have terms of 18–24 months, or 30–36 months for large projects. Construction loans have a floating interest rate that resets each month. LIBOR is a very common index, although sometimes lenders will use the prime rate. Loans typically had a spread of about 250 basis points over the one-month LIBOR, which meant that the rates on construction loans were about 3.8% in late 2017. This spread tends to not change much across different cities or states, meaning construction loan rates tend to be roughly the same across the country. Origination fees can vary from 0.5% to 1.0%. Nevertheless, city grants and local municipality sources are *critical* as gap filling sources. There is a wide variation across cities in terms of the funding and resources available to support construction of affordable housing. The lender/syndication will hire an architect to do monthly inspections; this cost will also be part of the project. Construction lenders want to see at least 15–20% of the LIHTC equity at the closing of an the construction loan—equity partnership. Lenders may also have a requirement for the amount of equity that is paid in by completion as opposed to how much is delayed and is dependent on a successful lease up and closing of the permanent loan.

While most students of real estate are familiar with the idea of sources and uses of funds in a development project, it is useful to consider two sets of sources and uses: permanent and for the construction period only. In other words, developers need to make sure they have access to sufficient funds to cover costs during construction, as well as after it is completed. This includes having sufficient reserves for various eventualities. For example, with the Federal HOME grants, 90% of the funds are disbursed up front, and the remaining 10% are disbursed when all the units are occupied. The developer of a project using HOME funds would need to keep this funding distribution process in mind, and have sufficient reserves available if the lease-up in does not go as planned.

There are concerns for both construction partners and permanent lenders that will be asked that developers will have to keep in mind. For example, they will need to know (1) the market for the units; (2) if the expenses are underwritten realistically, and (3) if all the funding sources are committed to the project. If these conditions are met, then the funds from the non-profit lender might be distributed. Figure 9.1 below shows an example of funding sources and uses for an actual affordable housing project in Madison. Notice that this project has five sources of funding, other than the deferred development fee.

Uses		Funding Sources	
Land/Site Utilities	$2,375,000	First mortgage	$6,900,000
Site Work	$400,000	City of Madison	$1,250,000
Construction	$12,850,000	FHLB	$1,016,901
Contingency	$665,000	Enterprise Loan	$200,000
Architect/Engineer	$370,000	Deferred Development Fee	$649,570
Interim/Construction	$500,000	Tax Credit Equity	$10,483,529
Permanent Financing	$395,000		
Soft Costs	$320,000		
Syndication costs	$5,000		
Development fee & OH	$2,100,000		
Reserves/Lease-up	$520,000		
Total uses	$20,500,000	Total sources	$20,500,000

Fig. 9.1 Example of funding uses and sources for an affordable housing project

Conclusion

In the next chapter, we move beyond the "nuts and bolts" of development and discuss the nuances of the affordable housing development process. Because of the large numbers of players and constituents involved, often with opposing interests, the process can quickly become a delicate balancing act, whereby the developer needs to be a successful people manager and skilled negotiator. Much of this knowledge is hard to come by in a textbook and can only be gained through years of experience. After having extensive discussions with policy makers, local government officials, and industry professionals, we feel like we can offer some guidance on some of the critical aspects of taking a project from conception to completion. Thus Chap. 10 will provide useful information (from both the public and private sides) for aspiring developers.

References

Community Reinvestment Act (CRA) (1977) P.L. 95–128, 91 Stat. 1147, title VIII of the Housing and Community Development Act of 1977, 12 U.S.C. § 2901

Opportunity Finance Network. What are CDFIs? Retrieved from https://ofn.org/what-cdfi

Chapter 10
Beyond Financing: The Process of Development

Abstract It is often said that real estate is a people business. Whether you are a broker or an investor, it is incredibly beneficial to have effective communication skills, ability to establish rapport and trust with other people, and have an extensive network of clients and colleagues. But if real estate is a "people business", then real estate development is the ultimate people business. A successful developer needs to maintain and manage a large and diverse network of professionals, including their internal team, architects, contractors, lawyers, lenders, local government officials, neighborhood associations, current and potential tenants, and others. This, of course in addition to understanding the "nuts and bolts" of the development process, such as being able to understand feasibility, relevant laws, and regulations, financing, construction, leasing, and marketing. While most of this book is dedicated to this "nuts and bolts" side of development, we want to emphasize that the "people" aspect is equally important. To that end, this chapter focuses on the nuances of affordable housing development that are typically not described in textbooks and are customarily learned through years of experience.

Developer's Perspective

One of the most important lessons any developer must learn early in their career is that they can only succeed if they satisfy many distinct constituencies, each with its objectives and interests. These constituencies include city planning commissions, zoning boards, neighborhood groups, fire and police departments, businesses, and others. Therefore, a developer first needs to identify all the major parties whose implicit or explicit will be required for the project to go ahead. Next, they need to understand the motivations and objectives of each party. Again, the various groups' interests may not be the same. For example, a significant employer may want to see lots of new construction of affordable housing in a particular area, but residents of that area may be completely opposed to the idea, citing a potential increase in traffic and strain on public services. Alternatively, residents of a specific neighborhood may welcome a new multifamily project, but the police department may raise objections, claiming the project would increase crime.

Whatever the specific groups and conflicts may be, the developer needs to be proactive in addressing potential objections. For example, in the United States, development projects are discussed in public meetings of area residents or neighborhood associations, and often put to the vote. Strong opposition by a majority of residents can kill a project. To avoid this problem, the developer can preempt common objections by addressing them beforehand. For example, the developer can gain the support of the police department by discussing their plans with them first. If the police department has objections or makes recommendations, the developer can win the support of the department by either implementing those recommendations or by explaining why it does not make sense to do so. For example, the developer might be planning to buy a building that is an eyesore or has a high concentration of crime, demolish it, and build something else on the site. Most people in the neighborhood may be happy to be rid of this "known cancer", but may still be concerned about the "unknown cancer" that may replace it. In such cases, the developer would increase the chance of neighborhood approval by having a specific, credible plan to deal with the crime issue. Naturally, they would work with the local police department to create this plan. Most police departments in the United States apply practices promoted by Crime Prevention Through Environmental Design (CPTED). Developed by criminologist C. Ray Jeffery (1971), who followed on earlier work by Elizabeth Wood, Jane Jacobs, and Schlomo Angel, CPTED is a theory of preventing crime by designing the built environment (particularly in urban areas). So if the proposed plan has features that would not minimize the chances of crime or increases them, then police departments can recommend that the developer changes some specific aspects of the plan.

Similarly, the developer can maximize the chances of the city planning commission's support by discussing their ideas with them early. Every urban site has a story, and the developer must know it. They must first understand for themselves and then convince the neighborhood and city officials why they are the right person to deal with the site. If it is a vacant site—why is it vacant? What, if anything, is wrong with it? If it is occupied—you must be buying because you are getting a deal on it. What are you going to do with it? All this advance work will strengthen the proposal, and makes it easier to defend against criticism, including during public discussions. Furthermore, even if the neighborhood association ends up opposing the project, consulting the city beforehand will make it more likely that the project ultimately goes ahead despite residents' opposition.

Another point to keep in mind is that developers should try to discreetly buy or option a site for a future project before other developers also get interested and bid up the price. Because once the owner of a vacant site realizes that there is keen interest from developers, they may raise the asking price significantly. This will likely erase any future profits that the developer was hoping to earn. A good rule of thumb is: "If you are a developer, and are buying a site because it is listed, you missed the opportunity. You need to get to the owner before it is listed."

Aspiring developers need to be aware that affordable housing takes much longer than market rate housing. From the conception of an idea to finding the right site, gaining the neighborhood and city's support, securing financing, applying for tax credits, securing all the permits, and finally doing the construction—the entire process can take twice as long as the process for market-rate housing. Furthermore, affordable housing for the elderly, for people with special needs and for the homeless require additional services, which requires contacts and partnerships that market-rate projects do not. Besides, some, if not all, tenants in affordable housing projects will pay only 30% of their incomes for rent. The rest will come from government agencies. So developers specializing in affordable housing need to establish and maintain contacts with relevant officials in the Department of Housing and Urban Development, and state local housing authorities.

Madison and Local Need

In this section, we reveal issues we discussed with significant parties involved in typical affordable housing: the city government and neighborhood associations. It is not uncommon that Midwestern cities will have a Housing Initiatives Specialist or an office that is tasked with this area of services. There are several states where these types of municipal offices will be particularly attuned to the Tax Increment Financing (TIF) program, such as Illinois, Colorado, New Mexico, Iowa, and Wisconsin. Although these programs are state-level programs, they are administered through municipal governance.

In mid-sized cities, it is not uncommon for single-family homes to provide a high percentage of the property tax base, even as much as 55%. Multifamily and office spaces would then give a smaller portion of the tax base. Importantly, in some cases, commercial office spaces only provide 25% of the property tax base, rather low for an urban municipal tax base.

As an urban planner, one needs to be keen to highlight that the significant challenge of the city is to deliver cost-efficient high-quality services to single-family homes. Consider two cities, Madison and Minneapolis, for example. One city could, in theory, compete with the other by lowering the taxes on commercial real estate in order to attract more office space investment and therefore increase the proportion of property tax base paid by commercial spaces. However, we should be aware that the decades-long approach of these municipal areas has been to provide a high quality of life, and not worry as much about competing with comparable urban areas on prices. Even if there were a cut in the costs for the city, in exchange for a lower tax rate, the city savings for property tax would be negligible. Furthermore, in states where there are TIF programs, a lower tax rate or smaller tax base would reduce the city's ability to use TIF. Hence, cities have found that there is a better strategy: specifically, refine the process for applying and receiving funds—or for getting approval for projects.

The most significant problems for midsized Midwestern cities are cost related. Demand is high for local housing, and considering ideal locations is critical. However, cost is increasing dramatically, and people are getting priced out of their neighborhoods. Furthermore, it is challenging to put up new housing in certain parts of cities, to expand residential zones, or shift the density of residential zones, because of the zoning regulations.

Municipal policies are designed to keep specific aspects of urban environs the same. For example, a few historic areas cannot be built upon. But also, re-zoning parts of a city can prove challenging as well. Finding the balance of increased density while maintaining the character of the neighborhood is difficult. *How do we know if a community needs more housing?* It could come from a developer-driven initiative (market driven). We could also look at rental data (low vacancies) if housing prices are going up in that area. Very rarely are the projects neighborhood-based or neighborhood driven.

Many mid-sized cities are divided neighborhoods, which are represented in local government by Alders, and have their own Neighborhood Associations (NA). But the problem with this structure of shared governance is that it is driven to favor full-time residents who have the free time to attend the NA meetings. The system eliminates the participation of many short-term residents or even long-term residents who are second and third shift workers. Feedback also favors current residents over potential residents, giving upper-class homeowners the power over developments that might be intended to serve low-income residents. Typically, out of 100 people, one third want new construction, one-third are concerned about change, and about one-third care about information on the development only. Furthermore, those numbers shrink over subsequent meetings with the NA. Hence, developers frequently do not have a good sense of what the community thinks, although the reigning opinion is that the most vigorous objections seem to be centered from NA, and therefore they are a critical step in the approval process for a project.

There has been a substantial criticism of the Section 42 housing over time, although we should highlight that the common criticism that it reduces property values in the adjacent areas is not correct and does not match the data that we have from city level studies.

How long does the development process take? Typically, the process, including the proposal, applying for the tax credits, and land use approvals, takes at least 2 years. Tax credits are the most extensive tool to deliver affordable housing. There are five main steps to this process.

Step 1: Proposal call goes out from the municipal government (July, for example). The developer meets with the city and establishes access to potential affordable housing funds. If feasible, they proceed.

Step 2: Meet with the Neighborhood Association and the Alder. This meeting is predominantly informational (1 month later).

Step 3: Formally apply to the city for the funds. These funds may also include HOME, CBG, bonds, and loans. Hopefully, this step consists of the Funding approval stage. Approval differs by governance structure—August (state funds), late November early December (City—for tax credits), February (dissolve).

Step 4: Now, enter land use approval process with the city. Architects design and propose a model to the Neighborhood Association and the Alder to refer plan for approval. Only Urban design districts have restrictions, but these are just in specific areas. Make a case for no undue burden. Typically, there is conditional use (about 1 year in).

Step 5: Approval requires about 40 conditions. Submit the design to fire department, apply to the state department of natural resources, to ensure that they are not going to put the building on wetlands. Fall break building ground, open in summer.

In this process, it is not abnormal for the cities to only enter at step three in the process, and for communities not receive their tax credit requests. Therefore, communities and developers must plan for all possible outcomes.

The advantage to tax credit developers is that they require very little equity, but they still need capital.[1] The capital investment is used to establish site control. They would also require capital investment to insure against the risk associated with the development of a site. All this said midsized Midwestern cities offer several positives for potential developers.

The positive aspects of the City of Madison are best summarized through the inclusion of excellent communication models and the reinforcement of best practices. Madison communicates well with developers about what they want. The city uses the requests for proposals period to be very specific about their desires for a particular site in the city. For example, downtown wants to see information in the research of the development about the potential of the tax base increasing. In more suburban office parks, jobs are a more significant concern.

Another unique aspect of City of Madison's approach to affordable housing has to do with financing. It is possible to use the last year of increment from high-end buildings downtown to push it back out into the affordable housing model. In other words, the city funds its affordable housing developments through the higher end developments. From an economic viewpoint, this is similar to a lump-sum transfer from developers that build high-end buildings to affordable housing developers. The economic intuition behind such transfer is that high-end buildings exert a negative externality in terms of housing affordability at the neighborhood level.

Open-minded city administrators are always looking to identify other cities' outstanding best practices and adopt them. Madison, WI is not an exception. Among other things, the City's Housing Strategy Committee is tasked with studying other cities' effective policies and programs with respect to housing. For example, the City of Madison has a rule that a landlord may not discriminate against people who do not currently have a residential address—an idea adopted from another city. However, some of the new, creative policies that the City adopted have been superseded by state law. Hence, it is critical that students, developers, industry experts, academics, and public officials are up on the current policies.[2]

---

[1] It would not be typical for young students and researchers to put forward these proposals, as the process for their approval is quite competitive.

[2] For example, see: Tenant Resource Center. 2017. Discrimination. Available online @ http://www.tenantresourcecenter.org/discrimination

Our research suggests that there are several best practices that could be included in state policy which might improve the situation in the municipal structures. For example, we should reconsider the potential benefits of inclusionary zoning. The state of Massachusetts has found that inclusionary zoning is a helpful tool in many midsized urban areas. For example, the City of Cambridge, MA has inclusionary zoning practices that they put in place to ensure that necessary laborers, such as firefighters and public educators, as well as other public employees, would be able to afford housing in the city.[3] Furthermore, mixed financing can provide many solutions for developers. Our research advocates a healthily mixed usage of tax-exempt state bonds, paired with Section 42 (LIHTC) transactions, adding TIF financing on top of this package, hypothetically. Since the state would be paying based on the scale of the development, this model would theoretically give the state more control but would cut costs for the developer. We also believe that more could be done to advocate for affordable housing, to show that every community could have it. Specific communities restrict affordable housing permits to 50 units per year, and, with a bit of heavy-handed state intervention, some of these policies could be changed. For example, about Shorewood Hills, exclusionary zoning was forced open to inclusionary zoning split 50/50 between owners and renters on a mandate from the state. The significant innovation and motivation of Housing Initiatives Specialists in these circumstances such as this, are to contribute to the development of the city. We see the best contributions of these offices as coordination and being proactive in the implementation of development models, pushing for policy and creating the programs to follow up on that policy.

At the County Level

This final section discusses the involvement of the county government in affordable housing. Here we focus on Dane County, which is the second largest county in the State of Wisconsin. It has seen constant growth in population since its founding in 1836. Currently it has population of nearly 520,000 residents.

The Dane County Board of Supervisors consists of 37 individual seats that represent each district based on population, who are elected in a non-partisan election on the first Tuesday of each April. Currently, Sharon Corrigan, of Middleton, is the chair of the board, overseeing a sizeable countywide apparatus that

---

[3]The City of Madison has not had Inclusionary Zoning (IZ) since a "sunset clause" went into effect in 2009. See: Inclusionary Zoning Advisory Oversight Committee. 2008. *Inclusionary Zoning Annual Report: And Proposals for Improvements to the Inclusionary Zoning Program*. City of Madison. For a positive take on inclusionary zoning see: Kautz, Barbara Ehrlich. 2001. In Defense of Inclusionary Zoning: Successfully Creating Affordable Housing. *University of San Francisco Law Review*. 36: 971–1032. See also: Kontokosta, Constantine E. 2014. Mixed Income Housing and Neighborhood Integration: Evidence from Inclusionary Zoning Programs. *Journal of Urban Affairs*. 36 (4): 716–741.

includes more representatives than many county boards across the country, including those in much more populated areas. For example, Orange County, in the State of California, only has five supervisors. What this means for Dane County is that the nature of shared governance is much more evenly divided among the residents of the county than in these other examples. The plurality ensures that they have the staff to maintain many standing committees.

The county government in Dane County is made up of many standing committees, committees of the county board, boards and commissioners, departments, and elected Offices. Necessarily, these committees are the concern of the developer, and a developer would need to be willing to learn how they function to work with them.

Any proposal would also have to go before the Zoning and Land Regulation Committee in the initial stages. If the plan involves several areas, it could go through the board. The developer needs to establish who has the rights to the land that they wish to develop on first. They will have to know if the tract is under the purview of the City of Madison, or whether it falls under the governance of the county board.

Once the land rights and jurisdiction have been established, the developer should proceed to communication with the proper local administrators. A developer would have to work with the local county officials, generally, if the tract of land that the developer wants to develop was in a town or area outside a municipal district. Ultimately, jurisdiction is determined by the zoning of the ground as well, so it is essential to consider zoning regulations.

Developers will also have to be willing to work with each of the following standing committees: Environmental, Agriculture & Natural Resources; Health & Human Needs; Personnel & Finance; Public Protection & Judiciary; Public Works & Transportation; and Zoning & Land Regulation. Individuals work on these committees as part-time jobs, whereas the developer works their position much more closely to a full-time position, so they will have to be aware of the nature of that position in their interactions.

The operating budget of the county is essential in determining several factors of the development process. In the case of Dane County, the operating budget is $587.1 million, and the capital budget is $50.6 million. The nature of these budgets determines the county tax rate. There will also be city, state and federal tax rates to consider, but the county tax rate is additionally vital for studying features of Tax Incremental Financing (TIF; see Chap. 4). In Dane County, the tax rate is $3.13 for every $1000 in value. This is part of the equation for the TIF program that we would need to consider, as TIF would be a combination of the county real estate tax, along with the city terms that would be established as well.

One consideration for the county governance is that TIF would potentially temporarily divert funds away from the county budget, the technical college, and the local K-12 public school district. Locals who are already residents in the area may take issue with this. Hence, coming forward with an efficient proposal that the county board can agree with is critical to the process of creating a smooth development. Health and Human Services is 51.55% of the total budget, while Public Safety and Criminal Justice is 19.22% of the operating budget. Therefore, convincing the county that the portions they are spending on these two features of the budget will decline if they are willing to finance housing, is a substantial consideration, and a potentially compelling argument that a developer can make.

From the perspective of county governance, communities critically need to address the issue of affordable housing. Employers need and want this development since a well-housed workforce is a workforce that functions better. The county's outreach platform, under the Dane County Housing Initiative (DCHI), offers extensive resources on general housing education, financing, down payment assistance programs, senior housing and assisted living, housing for the homeless, land use, policy, and planning tools for communities, and related topics. In addition, Access Dane, a publicly housed database, gives developers the tax assessments of every single real property, for both land and improvements. Developers will have to check the years of the evaluations, and then visit a listing service, such as MLS or Zillow, to find comparable near the plot that they would like to develop. Hence, developers could use these resources in their preparations for establishing site control, a necessary step before the tax credit or TIF application processes (see Chaps. 3 and 4). A researcher can also find existing developers on the website for DCHI developers and should be aware that most communities have assessors who find the land costs. They note that, because of county-level regulations, tax credit projects developed in rural areas might be incentivized to go 100% affordable in rural areas.

References

Inclusionary Zoning Advisory Oversight Committee (2008) Inclusionary zoning annual report: and proposals for improvements to the inclusionary zoning program. City of Madison

Jeffery CR (1971) Crime prevention through environmental design. Sage, Beverly Hills, CA

Kautz BE (2001) Defense of inclusionary zoning: successfully creating affordable housing. Univ San Francisco Law Rev 36:971–1032

Kontokosta CE (2014) Mixed income housing and neighborhood integration: evidence from inclusionary zoning programs. J Urban Affairs 36(4):716–741

References

Alonso W (1960) A theory of the urban land market. Pap Reg Sci 6(1):149–157
Briffault R (2010) The most popular tool: tax increment financing and the political economy of local government. Univ Chicago Law Rev 77:65–95
Capps K (2017) Tracking the shadow of public housing budget cuts. City Lab. Available https://www.citylab.com/equity/2017/04/tracking-the-shadow-of-public-housing-budget-cuts/521778/. Accessed 4 Nov 2017
Casella A (1999) The role of market size in the formation of jurisdictions. Rev Econ Stud
Cassell MK, Turner RC (2010) Racing to the bottom? The impact of intrastate competition on tax abatement generosity in Ohio. State Local Gov Rev 42(3):195–209
Center on Budget and Policy Priorities (2016) Cuts in federal assistance have exacerbated families' struggles to afford housing. Available https://www.cbpp.org/research/housing/chart-book-cuts-in-federal-assistance-have-exacerbated-families-struggles-to-afford. Accessed 4 Dec 2016
Center on Budget and Policy Priorities (2011) Section 8 rental assistance programs are not growing as share of HUD budget. Available https://www.cbpp.org/research/section-8-rental-assistance-programs-are-not-growing-as-share-of-hud-budget. Accessed 4 Dec 2016
Chetty R, Hendren N, Kline P, Saez E (2014) Where is the land of opportunity? The geography of intergenerational mobility in the United States. Q J Econ 129(4):1553–1623
Ciochetti B, Malizia E (2000) The application of financial analysis and market research to the real estate development process. In: DeLisle JR, Worzala E (eds) Essays in honor of James A. Graaskamp: ten years after. Springer, Boston, MA, pp 135–163
Confessor, Nicholas (2018) Congestion pricing plan dies in Albany. New York Times
Council of Development Finance Agencies (2015) Tax increment finance state-by-state report
de Leeuw F, Ekanem NF (1971) The supply of rental housing. Am Econ Rev 61(5):806–817
DeLisle J, Griego R (2008) Frontdoor/Backdoor analysis. Case study, The University of Washington
Desmond M (2016) Evicted: poverty and profit in the American City. Crown Publishers, New York
Dokow E, Luque J (2018) Provision of local public goods in mixed income communities. J Hous Econ. https://doi.org/10.1016/j.jhe.2018.02.005
Dougherty C (2018) California housing problems are spilling across its borders. New York Times
Dye RF, Merriman DF (2006) Tax increment financing: a tool for local economic development. J Hous Community Dev 63(3):22
Glaeser EL (2011) Triumph of the city: how our greatest invention makes us richer, smarter, greener, healthier, and happier. Penguin Press, New York
Glaeser EL, Gyourko JE (2008) Rethinking federal housing policy: how to make housing plentiful and affordable. AEI Press, Washington DC

Glaeser EL, Gyourko JE (2003) The impact of building restrictions on housing affordability. Econ Policy Rev 9(2):21–39

Graaskamp JA (1972) A rational approach to feasibility analysis. Apprais J 40:513–522

Graaskamp JA (1981) Fundamentals of real estate development. The Urban Land Institute, Washington, DC

Graaskamp JA, Jarchow SP (1991) Graaskamp on real estate. The Urban Land Institute, Washington, DC

Green RK, Malpezzi S (2003) A primer on us housing markets and housing policy, AREUEA Monograph Series. Urban Institute Press, Washington, DC

Gyourko J, Mayer C, Sinai T (2013) Superstar cities. Am Econ J Econ Policy 5(4):167–199

Hu W (2017) New York's tilt toward congestion pricing was years in the making. New York Times

Hu, Winnie and Jesse McKinley (2018) Congestion pricing plan for Manhattan Ran into politics. Politics won. New York Times, Sep 4

Inclusionary Zoning Advisory Oversight Committee (2008) Inclusionary zoning annual report: and proposals for improvements to the inclusionary zoning program. City of Madison

Ingraham AT, Singer HJ, Thibodeau TG (2005) Inter-city competition for retail trade: can tax increment financing generate incremental tax receipts? Available SSRN https://ssrn.com/abstract=766925 or https://doi.org/10.2139/ssrn.766925. Accessed 22 July 2005

Jacobs J (1961) The death and life of great American cities. Vintage, New York

Jeffery CR (1971) Crime prevention through environmental design. Sage, Beverly Hills: CA

Joint Center for Housing Studies of Harvard University (2017). The state of the nation's housing: Harvard University

Kautz BE (2001) In defense of inclusionary zoning: successfully creating affordable housing. Univ San Francisco Law Rev 36:971–1032

Kontokosta CE (2014) Mixed income housing and neighborhood integration: evidence from inclusionary zoning programs. J Urban Aff 36(4):716–741

Lefcoe G, Swenson CW (2014) Redevelopment in California: the demise of TIF-funded redevelopment in california and its aftermath. Natl Tax J 67:719–744

Luque J (2018) Assessing the role of TIF and LIHTC in an equilibrium model of affordable housing development. Reg Sci Urban Econ. https://doi.org/10.1016/j.regsciurbeco.2018.06.005

Malpezzi S (2015) The Wisconsin program in real estate and urban land economics: a century of tradition and innovation. University of Wisconsin-Madison, Madison

Malpezzi S, Green RK (1996) What has happened to the bottom of the us housing market? Urban Stud 33(10):1807–1820

Manasseh T (2017) We are reclaiming Chicago one corner at a time. New York Times

Maslow AH (1943) A theory of human motivation. Psychol Rev 50(4):370

Mathews J (2017) California's housing crisis is spreading to other states. San Francisco Chronicle

McDonald JF (2015) Affordable housing: an economic perspective. Architecture_MPS 7(3):1–16

Mesch S (2017) County Board approves using former Messner property to create affordable housing. Wisconsin State J

Mills ES (1967) An aggregative model of resource allocation in a metropolitan area. Am Econ Rev 57(2):197–210

Muth, R., 1969. Cities and housing: the spatial patterns of urban residential land use. University of Chicago, Chicago, 4, pp. 114–123

O'Sullivan A (2012) Urban economics. McGraw-Hill/Irwin, New York

Olsen EO (1969) A competitive theory of the housing market. Am Econ Rev 59(4):612–622

Paulsen K (2015) Housing needs assessment: Dane County and municipalities. Report prepared for: Dane County health and human needs committee, Dane County Department of Human Services and Dane County Planning and Development Department

Quigley JA, Raphael S (2004) Is housing unaffordable? why isn't it more affordable? J Econ Perspect 18(1):191–214

Reese P (2017) California exports its poor to Texas, other states, while wealthier people move in. Sacramento Bee

References

Safire W (2009) Location, Location, Location New York Times, 29 June

Schwartz A (2010) Housing policy in the United States, 2nd edn. Routledge, New York

Sirmans GS, Benjamin JD (1991) Determinants of market rent. J Real Estate Res 6(3 (Fall 91)):357

Soglin P, O'Keefe J, Wallinger S, Rhodes L (2013) Annual report on homeless persons served in dane county. City of Madison, Madison

Tenant Resource Center (2017) Discrimination. Available http://www.tenantresourcecenter.org/discrimination

Tighe JR, Mueller EJ (eds) (2013) The affordable housing reader. Routledge, New York

Treasury US (2014) Low-income housing tax credits: affordable housing investment opportunities for banks. Community Development Insights

Uhler B, Garosi J (2018) California losing residents via domestic migration. Legislative Analyst's Office, Sacramento, CA

U.S. Department of Housing and Urban Development (2007) Fair market rent: overview

Vance JD (2016) Hillbilly Elegy. Harper Press, New York

Weber R (2013) Tax increment financing in theory and practice. Financing economic development in the 21st century, 53, p 55

Whyte WH (2012) City: rediscovering the center. University of Pennsylvania Press, Philadelphia, PA